HONORING THE ANCESTORS

Honoring the Ancestors
A Basic Guide

Galina Krasskova

SANNGETALL PRESS

Featured on the cover (from left to right, top to bottom):

Karl Dabravalskas with his son John Paul Dabravalskas
Jane Butler
Hugh Shoff and Lucinda Shoff (née Hefner)
Ursula Dabravalskas (née Blasis), Julia Wagner (née
Dabravalskas), Karl Dabravalskas, and John Dabravalskas
Linnie Hanna (née Shoff)
John Dabravalskas (right before WWII)
Mary Ann Dabravalskas (née Hanna)
John Dabravalskas (Korean War)

All photos are from the collection of the author.

Sanngetall Press Valknot design by K.C. Hulsman

Dedication

This book is dedicated to all of our ancestors,
and to Mitochondrial Eve, ancient mother of us all,
and to all those who seek to honor their dead.

May we restore the balance.
May we take up again those ancient threads,
May we undo the depredations of generations,
and may our traditions flourish anew.

Acknowledgements

I would like to thank my god daughter Boo, who always reminds me to tend to children's spirits too, and to my partner Sannion, for putting up with me in my enthusiasms and not letting me get too far off track. I'd also like to thank my friends Mary Ann Glass and Allen Paiva, who have accompanied me on many an ancestral pilgrimage; K. C. Hulsman, for her ongoing support; Laura Patsouris who helped me and inspired me to grow as an ancestor worker; and all those who took the various iterations of my 'Honoring the Ancestors' class---I learned so much from each of you! I'd also like to thank my amazing colleague Dver who formatted this book and did all the graphics magic to make it happen. This book literally would not exist without her expertise. Thank you all.

Finally, I want to thank my ancestors, biological and adopted. Without you, I would not stand. Without you, I would not be. Thank you for supporting me, nourishing me, and carrying me through sometimes in spite of myself. I am humbled and grateful to carry you all at my back. Ashe!

Contents

ištverme

It's a hard people that birthed me
hard and unyielding
like weathered stone
 hungry flame,
the bones of the dead,
hard like the yoke
of occupation
and the necessary brutality
of resistance.

It's hard soil
that holds them,
concealing bones
of an ancient nation,
lands devastated
by generations
and horrors
only the stones themselves
might recount
and they are silent.

It's a hard God that took me up
and He made me hard in His loving.
There's a hard war to be fought.
and I'll take point.
My ancestors nod grimly
when I say this.
They know
all the different permutations
of grit.
Just try to break them.
They never yield--
never forgot their ceremonies either.
They know from whence
their power comes.

My people,
children of fire
born under a blazing northern sun
know the secret of endurance.
We keep our power hidden.
We keep our borders close.
We guard what must be guarded.
These things come down in the blood
like hard edged steel.
Then like steel we rise.

Opening Ancestor Prayer Given at the May 10, 2012 UN Conference on Women and Indigeny

Let us begin our work today by calling upon our ancestors.

Let us call upon the Algonquin, the Wappingers Confederacy and all other Native peoples who walked this land and whom this land remembers.

Let us begin by calling upon the mothers and fathers, grandmothers and grandfathers of our lines, all the way back to the time our respective peoples began.

Let us begin by reaching into the past, to the strength and wisdom of our forebears, for guidance as we seek to transform our present.

I call now to our collective ancestors, women and men who laid down their lives, who faced conquest, struggle, potential obliteration, who stood strong and proud so that each of their descendants might have a chance at survival, at life, at continuance. I call to those men and women whose joys and sacrifices, struggles, and successes culminated in each one of us sitting here today. Hear us, oh honored dead.

Those of you who came before us, living lives rooted in your own ancestral ways, be with us here today. Be with us as we come together in dialogue and peace. Inspire us that from here, buoyed by the strength of our collective passion, our collective words, our collective insights, we might go forth and transform our oh-so-damaged world. Root us, oh ancestors, in our respective indigeny. Root us in the knowledge that indigeny is about celebrating the dignity of every living being on the planet; indigeny is about recognizing that we are indisputably connected to the earth, the land, and most of all to each other. Oh ancestors, let our work today honor that awareness with grace.

Oh our mothers, our fathers, our foremothers, our forefathers all the way back to the time of the beginning, are calling us to action. I know you all hear that call. May our warrior ancestors, who never, *ever* went gently into the good night of conquest, who fought and laid down their lives sometimes en masse for the survival of their traditions, our traditions, be with us, let us call upon them now. Defiant ones, proud and enduring ones, men and women both. Give us the strength to reject that which would poison and corrupt our connections to our ancestors, our Holy powers, the land upon which we live, and each other. Give us the wisdom to know in our bones that sustainability does not come from disconnected governments and avaricious corporations but from the belly of our ancestors and the traditions they called their own, traditions that are our birthright, our inheritance.

Oh Ancestors, give us the courage to confront privilege—our own most of all—to actively engage with ideas and concepts that may be painful, to engage with mindfulness, respect, and authenticity.

Most of all, let us never give up, never surrender, never step back from this fight; no matter what hostility or pressure we might face. We too are warriors in a struggle that has spanned generations. Stand with us, oh our beloved dead. Grant us a measure of your strength. We carry the medicine of our ancestors. Oh Ancestors, hear our vow: no one here will be legislated, educated, starved, murdered, shamed out of existence. We will not allow our traditions—whatever those ancestral traditions might be, for here we sit, from all corners of the globe united by a common purpose—to be forgotten. We will not allow the land that cradles the bones of our foremothers and forefathers to be devastated. Many things can be lost or taken by the rushing press of dubious progress, or through the violent devastation of conquest, but indigeny is not one of them. It flourishes in each one of us. It is in the soil upon which we walk. It is hidden in our skin and blood and bones, in the connection from parent to child to grandchild and beyond. Oh our mothers and fathers, grandmothers and grandfathers, help us stay consciously rooted in that knowledge.

May we hold strong. May our ancestors sustain us.

It will take both sides, living and dead, to right the balance of this world.

May we hold strong and never bow our heads in fear.

We are each our ancestral lines walking. The time is now and I call upon our ancestors: give us ears to hear and eyes to see and the courage to go fearlessly wherever we must go, to do whatever we must do, to protect and heal our broken world.

With the blessing of the ancestors—all of our collective and honored dead—may we be given strength and may we always remember: we do not do this work alone. We are our ancestral lines walking. We come with nations of our ancestors at our back. May they be honored. May they be hailed. May they be remembered. May they inspire us.

Introduction

"You are the product of a million hopes and dreams whispered into the darkness; the yearnings of hearts longing to be remembered for their life's work and the marks they left upon the Earth, among the people you stand with today."[1]

You hold in your hands a book that I have wanted to write for nearly a decade. Early on, it was impressed upon me first by the Gods and then by my own ancestors how important it is to restore our connection with our dead, how vitally important this is not only for the restoration of our polytheistic traditions, but for changing, healing, and restoring our world. It's been a long journey, one in which I've been at times alternately bitter and petulant, joyous and enthusiastic. Mostly, I never thought I would get here. This book has been a very long time in coming.

The basis for this book is an eight-week course that I taught four times from 2013-2014, largely because I saw the need. I've taken those eight lessons and structured this book around them and at the end of each chapter, you'll see suggestions on what you can do to help integrate the information in the chapter into your regular practice. People need to know how to honor their dead and I was seeing a lot of desire to do so but uncertainty about how to get started. This is understandable. It's not, after all, as though we have good models for this sort of thing in our everyday lives. (If you do, you're very, very lucky!) I myself had worked for at least ten years before I got my ancestor practices anywhere close to what they ought to be. It was a constant struggle, one that forced me to deal with a lot of hurt and resentment around my living relatives.

I kept up with it because I knew on some level--though at the time I never could have told one how--that it was important, really important, and I was fortunate to have some amazing guides in this work. Firstly, when I really started to get pushed to honor my dead, I had a roommate who practiced Lukumi and he took me to his elder who helped me get started cleanly. Then, when I already had a constant practice, I made the acquaintance of an amazing ancestor worker, who became a fast friend, and who helped me hone my ancestor work so that I could go even deeper into communication and veneration. I had really good models. That didn't mean that I didn't have to work my butt off, though, and there were times, many of them especially early on, that it was a bitter struggle.

I tell people with ancestor work to 'start where you start' and eventually it will all come full circle. We're not in this alone, after all. Our beloved dead have a vested interest in having us get this piece right and they'll help. More and more I think those first faltering steps aren't just a matter of having us learn to relate to them, but having them learn to relate to us as well and that's important. We're not in this alone. Getting the ancestor piece sorted out---getting one's ancestral house or court in order, as many ancestor workers might say---is one of the most crucial things you will ever do. I cannot overestimate the importance of this work. It is crucial to honor our dead.

As polytheists, we're engaged in a process of rediscovering, rebuilding, and restoring traditions long ago sundered and in many cases, violently destroyed. We are engaged in the process of restoring not only our religious traditions, but the cultural sensibilities that were inextricably bound up in the exercise of that ancient piety. The fragments that have come down to us are few, the opposition both conscious and unconscious great. We are creating roots for ourselves that our little portion of the World Tree might once again flower. It is a daunting task.

We are not alone in this work. I will say that again and again and again: our ancestors were there. They lived these traditions that we are struggling to resurrect. Some of them bear a heavy weight for abandoning those same traditions. That means they have an obligation to their descendants to put those sundered threads to right. The generation that, for whatever reason, made the decision to abandon their ancestral faiths, bears a tremendous burden. Call upon them. Let them have no peace, no rest, no honor, no strength, no rebirth, and no glory until they have made reparation. Call them out and demand their help. Our world is so out of balance that it's going to take both sides of the equation: living and dead working in tandem to put it right again. Our ancestors' connection with their dead, their commitment to venerate them, were powerful spiritual contracts. When these practices were abandoned, so were those ancient obligations. Our world is suffering for that each and every day.

Honoring the dead is all about finding balance and maintaining a stable life and spiritual practice and allowing that to inform every interaction with the world at large. This is the foundation. This is what mature, responsible, pious people do. It's part and parcel of maintaining a proper household. At least in the time of our ancestors it was. I write fiercely about this, because I feel so strongly the push of our ancestors and Gods to do this work in the here and now. Nor am I the first to advocate calling out those ancestors who abandoned their traditions. I learned to do this from a Dagara Elder and I've seen both Druid and Celtic practitioners doing the same. It's not an act of hate. It's a chance for them to cleanse their wyrd and undo some of the harm that came, ultimately, from the triumph of monotheistic hegemony. Big words, I know, and I promise I'll unpack some of this as we progress through the book you now hold, and well before we go and demand something of our dishonored dead[2] (and I can think of no greater dishonor than to abandon one's Gods regardless of the political expediency), we should focus first on establishing proper ancestral practices with the rest of them. That's what this book will teach.

Honoring the dead is simplicity itself. Simple does not necessarily mean easy, mind you. Sometimes establishing a good working relationship, based in love and respect can be the hardest thing in the world. Families are complicated. If someone has a difficult relationship with their immediate family that can make ancestral work very hard at first. The key to moving forward into practice is to remember that our ancestors are not just those of our immediate family who may have died. Our ancestral line stretches back to the beginning of time, to the moment the first quadruped pulled itself out of the primordial ooze and decided to see what life was like on land. We are but one pearl in a gleaming strand of pearls stretching back into those misty beginnings and onward into our future. That's a lot of dead people one can honor! If the immediate generations are difficult, go further back. We have our tribal mothers and fathers who watch over the entire ancestral line. The female dead especially, what the Norse call "Disir," are powerful and govern both the integrity and luck of one's line. Call upon them for help in getting started. Call upon the Gods and Goddesses of the underworld and bring them gracious gifts asking that They may help facilitate your relationship with your dead. Then, give it time and consistent effort. The dead are usually more than willing to meet us halfway, more than halfway if we're sincere in our practice.

I believe we are actually hard-wired to honor our dead. It's a very instinctual thing. In the most secular of cultures we do it naturally: naming children after our dead, displaying their photos, leaving flowers at cemeteries, setting up impromptu shrines where people, especially children, are killed, and in dozens of other little ways. We simply no longer put these things in a sacred context. Consciously honoring the dead takes this ingrained awareness one step further. That is the key to ancestor work: mindful attention. When we bring these practices out into the open, incorporating them into our daily lives we are taking a powerful step towards rebuilding our lost traditions. We are creating a bridge whereby our own ancestors, who have a vested interest in our success, can come forward and help us in our lives. That's a very powerful thing.

When it comes to restoring our polytheistic traditions, sometimes knowing where to begin to really make a difference is daunting. I say here, begin with your own dead. These were family traditions. They began in the hearts and minds of those gathered in the sacred shelter of home and hearth. Begin with your dead. Let the restoration begin with returning to the ancient practices of celebrating, reverencing, and caring for our beloved dead. Set out their pictures, light candles, set out offerings of food and drink, talk to them, share your victories and your sorrows however small with them, and ask for their protection. Ask for their guidance. Ask for their aid. Each and every single one of you has the capacity to do this work. You don't need any special psychic gifts, you just need to be human. Moreover, if you can find and maintain right relationship with your ancestors, they will teach you how to do so with the Gods and other Holy Powers. That is no small thing at all. We are all engaged in tradition building, in the slow, painstaking restoration of polytheistic religions and practices that were long ago thought consigned to a history determined by monotheistic dominance. So long as our ancestors exist however, those traditions are not lost. So long as our Gods grant us the favor of Their blessings and presence, we will not be silenced.

Now, go honor your dead.

Galina Krasskova
Beacon, NY
August 7, 2014

Notes:

[1]From sexgodsrockstars.wordpress.com/2014/01/16/ancestors-and-your-beloved-dead/

[2]That dishonor lies only with the first generation or two to convert. Our recent ancestors grew up in homes that had been monotheistic for generations. There is no dishonor for them in that they practiced the religion of their families, the religion of their birth. Many may even have established deep devotional ties to the Gods of their birth religions. That is fine. Honor them.

Chapter 1

In suppliciis deorum magnifici, domi parci, in amicos fideles erant.

They were, in offerings to the Gods lavish, at home frugal, in friendship faithful.

(Sallust)

I want to start by sharing with you a few traditional sayings about ancestor work:

"The souls of the dead are the protection of the living."
Lithuanian proverb

"We stand on the bones of our dead."
Lukumi proverb

"We stand on the shoulders of our ancestors."
Yoruba proverb

"Crown your ancestors."
Delphic Maxim

Among the ancient Romans, the very word from which we get our word 'religion' meant to tie oneself to the practices of one's ancestors. It was about tradition and the way in which ancestral remembrance and traditions sustained and carried one through into a rich, rewarding, and honorable life. This remains true today: this is our foundation. The traditions that we are working to restore and in which we must, of necessity, struggle to root ourselves are our most essential foundation from which everything else flows.

Every pre-Christian polytheist would have engaged in ancestor veneration of some culturally and religiously defined sort as a matter of course. It wasn't something reserved for spiritworkers or priests or shamans or any other specialist. It was what one did as a mature, responsible adult. Stepping into the full obligation of honoring the ancestors oneself was one of the defining facets of adulthood. It went without saying. Not just that, honoring your ancestors was what defined and determined family. It was what made you a part of your family. This even created legal precedent in the ancient world! There is an ancient Greek court case where a slave woman wins her freedom by recounting in court how she participated in the ancestor rites of her master's family. That was enough to make her part of that family. Ancestor veneration was also one of the first things that early

8

Christianity worked hard to eradicate (with varying degrees of success at first). I have my theories about why and most of them come down to this: if you know who you are and where you come from, if you are truly rooted in your ancestral lineage and power, if you know that every time you bow your head or speak your prayers your entire ancestral line does so with you, you cannot be spiritually corrupted.

Moreover, a lot of us today feel very isolated but if you're honoring your dead, you have this whole community, no matter where you are. You have people in your court, people who love you, care about you, who want you to succeed; and they'll support you as you support them.

Ancestor work is the single biggest commonality across indigenous cultures. We as polytheists are working to restore our indigenous religions: all the religions our ancestors practiced, replete with their Gods and spirits, before monotheism swept across the world. This is sacred work but I don't believe it can be done cleanly, wisely, or well, without the help of the ancestors. I've said again and again (and I'll be repeating it throughout this book) that it's going to take both sides of the equation---living and dead---to right the imbalances in our world, and to restore our broken, sundered, desecrated traditions. There's nothing more important that one can do than honor one's dead consistently.

I'm betting that some of you already honor your ancestors at least a little. I believe it's a very, very deeply ingrained thing, that we're hard-wired to make these connections. We visit graves, name children after our dead, tell their stories, and so forth. We may not culturally do it in a sacred context---that we've lost---but vestiges exist. If some of you were fortunate enough to grow up not in monotheisms but in your indigenous traditions, I'm betting there are sacred practices too. Have any of you ever gone into a Thai or Chinese restaurant and seen small altars with incense and maybe a sacred figure? Well, one of the things that the owners are doing with that is paying homage to their ancestors, every single day. Now, of course we don't want to copy anyone else's religious practices and in truth we don't need to. There was a time, long ago, when---regardless of from where your ancestors came---your people had cohesive, sacred, ancestral traditions too. We can reclaim those. We must. It's one of the most crucial parts of polytheistic restoration but more than that, it's one of the most spiritually and even physically nourishing things you can do for yourselves, your loved ones, and all those who will come after you. Ancestor work makes one's life better.

Before we go any farther, let's take a moment to clarity what is meant when we use the term 'ancestor.' It's really something of a catch-all term. There are many types of honored dead that can be classed as ancestors:

- ➢ ancestors by blood
- ➢ ancestors by adoption
- ➢ deceased friends
- ➢ deceased teachers, mentors, etc.
- ➢ those of your work lineage (as a diviner, I honor all the diviners who came before me; a computer programmer can honor all deceased computer specialists who preceded her; a doctor can honor any and all physicians who preceded him as part of his or her lineage ancestors)
- ➢ spirits of dead children in your line, aborted children, miscarried children
- ➢ groups of dead that you may feel called to honor (I specifically honor the military dead, for instance; someone I know honors the transgender dead as a special group, another specifically honors the dead of the deaf community, and in public rituals we all speak for them and give them space and reverence, bringing their stories and presence, their memories to life)
- ➢ your partner's/partners' dead (marriage or setting up a household with someone is a matter of joining ancestral lines over and above coming together in love---they don't tell you that in Emily-Friggin'-Post)

10

➢ personal or cultural heroes
➢ elemental powers (in many traditions the elements are our eldest ancestors)

There's no right or wrong place in which to start. Some of you may be wondering if you need any special psychic abilities or talents to do this work, if you have to be a medium or empath and the answer is no. Absolutely not. This is something everyone can do. Mediums may have a leg up on clear communication but they're specialists. You don't have to be a specialist to honor your dead. We all have dead. It's the one unifying, universal thing. It is right and proper that we honor them. Once we take those first stumbling steps, they'll meet us half way. They'll find ways to communicate. It might not be with words but they'll find a way and you will too. I've seen it happen over and over again. So don't doubt your ability. Everyone can do this. You'll each find your own unique way of engaging too within the framework you'll be learning.

As you get started, there are only a few taboos that I'd like you to remember and I think they're pretty easy. Most importantly, don't ever put a picture of a living person on your ancestor altar. It's considered disrespectful and 'courting death.' (I can think of only two exceptions to this and we'll touch on that in the chapter on setting up an ancestor shrine.) It literally marks the person as dead. Engage as consistently as possible. Be respectful. Those are pretty much the only 'rules' that you need to worry about right now. Your ancestors may eventually give you more involved guidelines as you deepen your connection to them, but that's something you'll work out with them as your practices evolve.

There is no one right way to do ancestor work. You're dealing with individuals. It's something that you will each have to discover and work out with your own ancestors as you go. As you progress through this book, you'll be given some tools to get you started but there is no cookie cutter model. Ancestor work is flexible because the ancestors aren't archetypes or metaphors; they're individuals, people with all the quirks that individual people have. Like any other relationship, the ones with your ancestors will take time and care to develop. Above all else, it helps to keep in mind that essentially, we are our entire ancestor lines walking.

SUGGESTIONS

Are there any customs for honoring the dead in your family, even if they're not specifically rooted in a 'religious' context? Talk to your relatives and see if you can come up with a couple of recipes, anecdotes, or family stories about ancestors. Start your own ancestor journal by writing them down.

Chapter 2

"Holy places are dark places. It is life and strength, not knowledge and words, that we get in them. Holy wisdom is not clear and thin like water, but thick and dark like blood."

(C.S. Lewis, Till We Have Faces)

This chapter is designed to give you some basic exercises that will help you develop whatever latent sensitivity to the dead you may have, that will teach you to meditate (we pray after all---talking to our dead---it's good to know how to listen too), and ways to center so that you can do this work mindfully. The exercises are, I will grant you, a little boring (at least I find them so) but they lead to overall psychic, emotional, and spiritual health when done regularly. You can even use them in your regular work day to cope with stress. I've taught them to business men and women for just that reason.

My friend Sophie Reicher has written an excellent little book called *Spiritual Protection*, where she gives a lot of these exercises too and I highly recommend it. In addition to learning those basics, we're also going to talk about our own indigeny: what that means and how we can reclaim our indigenous consciousness. That's a huge part of ancestor work too and fortunately, it becomes easier the more engaged with our ancestors we are. They really help strip away unhealthy filters from our eyes. The work itself rewires us and the way we see the world and that's a good thing.

I'm going to jump right into the exercises first. They're not at all difficult, I promise you, but they teach the mind to focus, to hit the appropriate meditative state where really good and productive communication can occur. I recommend doing them for a minimum of ten minutes a day. That's not too much (set a kitchen timer or stop watch if you want) and you will see results.

The first and most important exercises that one can do are grounding and centering. These two simple exercises are the backbone of any spiritual or esoteric practice. They are also, as noted above, extraordinarily useful for dealing with stress and tension. I've also found that they can be an effective tool in managing a bad temper! I learned how to center in a martial arts class, via a breathing exercise called the 'Four-Fold Breath,' which I shall present here. This is not a difficult exercise. All it takes is time. The breath pattern itself will center you. Centering is a multi-faceted process: it gives you breathing room to effectively act rather than react to what's happening around you; it pinpoints your actual, physical center; it helps you establish a personal boundary, to determine where you end and the outside world begins; it aligns the energetic and physical bodies so that both occupy the same space; and it helps one to cope with and effective process random emotions and energies to which one might be exposed throughout the day or the work.

To do this breathing exercise, simply inhale four counts, hold four counts, exhale four counts, hold four counts. Do this over and over for about ten minutes. You can do this anywhere. You have to breathe after all!

I recommend practicing this several times a day. The good thing about this exercise is that you can do it while going about your daily business and no one need be the wiser. I like to give myself a mnemonic to remind myself to practice. For instance, you might say "every time I see a silver car, I am going to center, ground, and check my personal shields." That would not be too frequent, by the way. The key is consistency and regularity of practice.

In time, as you breathe, you want to feel all the breath, all the random energies in your body gathering about three inches below the navel. Eventually, as you breathe, you want to feel the energy gathering in a glowing golden ball at this point. A student of mine once put it this way: "Basically, centering is 'contemplating your navel'!" She was right too. Be sure to breathe through your diaphragm taking deep, even breaths. Don't rush and don't worry if your mind wanders. Just gently bring it back to the breath. One caveat: large busted women and most men center higher, at the solar plexus and even sometimes in the heart chakra area. There is nothing esoteric about this; it's pure body mechanics and physiology. Find your physical center and that's where your esoteric center should also be. One's center is based on where one's center of gravity is. For most women, that is in the hips, the second chakra area. Some larger, or large busted women, and most men center at the solar plexus or in some cases even higher. Centering creates a necessary boundary; it demarcates where you begin and end and where the outside world begins and ends.

Now, once you're centered and once the energy in your body has been collected, it has to go somewhere. Grounding adds stability; it gives one a connection to the earth; it makes one strong, flexible, and resilient. Basically grounding is just sending all the energy/tension/emotions that have been collected in the body, down into the earth. (Science tells us that everything is energy in motion, which means tension, stress, emotions are energy too and energy can be worked with.) Don't worry if you can't see or feel anything....start with the mental focus and eventually your awareness of the internal flow of energy will increase.

The easiest grounding exercise to begin with is also, like centering, a breathing exercise. Inhale and feel the energy gathered in your center. Now, as you exhale, feel that energy exiting the body through the root chakra (the perianal area) or through the feet, though I find the root chakra is the more stable point. Some practices place the root right at the end of the tail bone---which is interesting after you've spent thirty years working it at the perineum. Try both and see which one works best for you. There are pros and cons to each method. Anyway, as you breathe, on the second exhale, feel it entering the earth and branching out into a thick, sturdy network of roots. Continue this imagery for as long as you need to, using each ensuing exhalation to take you further and further into the earth until you feel fully grounded. You can use this visualization and breathing technique to rid your body of tension, stress, even physical pain. I've used it to unknot spasming muscles, imagining that I was inhaling and exhaling through the knot itself.

Now, in time you will want to learn different ways of grounding, and you will find that many of the exercises are primarily visualization exercises. Now don't worry if you're not good at visualizing things...that too is a skill that comes in time. I always had difficulty with it. You may find that the image comes via feelings instead of sight and that's okay too. Just like people have different learning styles, some being visual, some auditory, some more kinesthetic in various combinations, the same holds true for meditation and energy work. As with ancestor work: start where you start.

Some people find it helpful to send energy down through the feet as they walk. That is a useful secondary grounding technique. The idea is that you're connecting yourself to something bigger than you are, and that something (the earth beneath your feet) can support and sustain you. It gives you a focal point upon which you are an axis. The standard idea with grounding is to be a tree. Once you've gathered the energy at your navel, send it down through the root chakra visualizing a tap root and rich network of smaller roots reaching deep into the earth. The root chakra is where one connects to the earth, to primal life energy. Send all the energy down, timing it to each exhalation, into the earth. See it streaming from your root chakra in a solid golden cord of energy. This cord goes down through the floor, through the foundations of the house and into the earth, it reaches very deeply and with each exhalation see it branching off like roots of a tree, tying you tightly to the earth.

These two exercises are pre-requisites to being able to shield effectively. The only requirement to gaining excellence is practice. As my Russian teacher told me when I was in high school: repetition is the mother of learning. That holds especially true here.

Some people balk at the idea of 'shielding.' It sounds harsh and divisive. In reality shielding is just about maintaining good boundaries, and you need personal boundaries to be a healthy human being and to maintain healthy relationships. A shield is a filter, one that you control, that helps in filtering out what is not you, all the stimuli that we face on a day to day basis. For people with strong psychic gifts it's a necessity and for people with lighter talents it's also a good and useful tool to have in one's metaphysical toolbox.

If you're poo-pooing the idea of energy work, then think of this as a mental exercise: visualize or imagine or feel a transparent wall, like plexiglass between yourself and others...try this in your job when a toxic co-worker or client (we all have them!) is harassing you: nothing they put off can penetrate. See if it makes a difference in how you come away from those stressful encounters.

Shielding is all about developing strong, flexible boundaries. I find that the people who have trouble maintaining good boundaries in other areas of their lives usually suck at shielding. They're also the ones who could benefit the most from it and who resist it the most fervently. I once actually had a client say to me: "I don't want to learn to shield. I want to be one with the universe." I'm afraid I was tired, aggravated, and a bit more blunt than I probably should have been: "Yeah, sweetheart. The universe is going to crush you like an empty beer can. Sit the fuck down and shield." But that's me: spreading diplomacy everywhere I go.

Perhaps it's best to think of a shield as a boundary or filter that you can strengthen or lighten or take down completely depending on the situation. One of the reasons it's so helpful is that it allows you to pinpoint what's you, what's an ancestor, what's Deity, what's white noise from the chaos in the minds around you, etc. It's also good, as I noted above, for stress. So how do you do it? Well, just as you send energy down through your ground, you can pull it up again. I would suggest centering, grounding and then pulling energy up on the inhalation and feeling it rise up around you fully encasing you. This is the most basic shield. Then you can tweak it to your own specifications. I do not recommend the new age 'white light' shield for the sole reasons that: (a) it's not very effective; and (b) it's very noticeable. Reicher gives quite a few different shielding techniques in her book and I recommend experimenting. You can even ask your ancestors for help.

While shielding is something of an advanced technique (I recommend focusing on centering and grounding for a few weeks first), one thing that everyone should do often and consistently is cleansing. It's very important when doing spiritual work to keep yourself spiritually and energetically clean. This is one of the ways that we can heighten our spiritual receptivity and what spiritworkers call 'signal clarity': the ability to receive (in whatever way it happens) and correctly recognize and interpret information, communication, and messages from the Gods, ancestors, and spirits.

There are dozens and dozens of ways to cleanse. The most common is probably a cleansing bath. (If you don't have a bathtub, don't worry. The really traditional way of doing a cleansing bath is to pour the mixture over your head. It's much more comfortable though to add stuff to a hot bath!) Here are a few of my favorites:

1. Add a can of dark beer to your bath. It totally cleanses the energetic body. (German folk custom)
2. One cup of apple cider vinegar, one cup of sea salt.
3. One cup of Florida Water.
4. Light a couple of bay leaves on fire and douse them in the bath water--my cleansing variation on *khernips*, a Greek form of lustral water used for purification.

You can also make up various combinations of herbs and add a little rum and call it a day. I recommend Cat Yronwode's book *Hoodoo Herb and Root Magic* because it gives appendices that list the spiritual usage of many different herbs and it's easy to mix and match. Usually the formula for most spiritual baths calls for three different ingredients and then a cologne like Florida Water, or rum, or ammonia or something like that. Play around and see what works best. I like cinnamon, frankincense, allspice, a bit of orange water and a dash of rum as a good blessing bath. All those herbs are associated with good fortune and wealth and spiritual abundance.

But really, pour some beer in your bath and call it a day if this is troubling to you. I would also suggest showering and changing your clothes as soon as you come in from work. We pick up an awful lot of psychic and energetic gunk in our work day. It's best to be clean from it as soon as possible. That along with the centering, grounding, and shielding exercises are what I consider the fundamentals to clean spiritual work.

Now, one other thing I wanted to begin exploring in this chapter was the idea of reclaiming one's own indigeny. 'Indigenous' is an adjective drawn from a Latin word that means 'native to, to be born of.' Some time ago, someone said

19

to me in a Facebook discussion that "I'm not really interested in 'traditions.' I'm interested in What Is. If a tradition varies from What Is, that tradition is WRONG and should be corrected" (emphasis not mine).

This is actually an interesting statement. I've heard this, in various permutations, quite a bit from non-polytheistic pagans. It makes me suspect that it's not just the veneration of many gods that is difficult for some folks, it's the entrenchment in a tradition with all the continuity, hierarchy, intergenerational transmission of praxis, etc., that entails. It's the very concept of spiritual lineage, of responsibility to something other than oneself. The Roman orator and statesman Cicero gave a definition and etymology of 'religion' that linked it directly to a Latin word meaning 'to bind.' Fleshing that out, he specifically meant it as 'being bound to the traditions of one's ancestors.' In his context, tradition implied ritual praxis and spiritual structure. (I'll spare you the further exegesis on Roman religious concepts and Latin etymology). I think it's precisely that responsibility---to oneself, one's community and land, to one's Gods and ancestors, to those that will come after us---that may be the issue. Progress isn't, to a polytheist, if it doesn't serve all of those things.

Mostly I was struck by the immediate certainty that it's the tradition that needs to be corrected. (Because something that is 'new' and untested must of course be superior to that which has worked organically for thousands upon thousands of years and more generations than anyone can count). This highlights yet another defining facet of polytheists: tradition is sacred to us. It is not something to cast away (as that generation of our ancestors who grasped at monotheism did) because doing so might be convenient, or seemingly easy, or might bring ease, leisure, and wealth to a few. (Not that there's anything wrong with convenience, leisure, and wealth when it comes from clean sources!) We long ago realized that modern life and our ancestral traditions are not exclusionary. Indeed our lives are enhanced by our commitments to our traditions and our Gods.

There is nothing inherently impossible about living in

the 21st century and being a devout polytheist. Perhaps we define 'progress' differently. Certainly, the beauty of a tradition rooted in ancestral wisdom is that it evolves and encompasses each age into which it is carried. I examine tradition, yes, because like most polytheists, I grew up in a monotheistic culture and I too am still learning how to restore and revive and live my traditions today (a thing that's not always comfortable at first---there's always a process of internal examination and sometimes deconstruction of old assumed tropes that occurs in tandem with this work), but I outright question this obsessive fetishization of modernity, of 'enlightenment' of 'progress.' It almost seems like a strange type of manifest destiny. I wonder if it doesn't come from one of our ancestral wounds, something we will address in depth in Chapter 5.

Our culture and society doesn't really prepare us for real spiritual engagement. Sometimes people have a sense, an experience with the Gods, a mystical opening and lacking the cultural framework for it, it breaks something vital in them with regard to spirituality. When you have those experiences hard on their heels comes a choice: you can look at the world around you and the order that has dominated us for 2000 years and say "This is not natural. It's wrong. It needs to be changed." Or you can break, shatter, crumble under the cognitive disconnect of being plunged right into the space that leads to those ancestral traumas. Or you can turn around and attack that which you experienced and all the rich and fertile places to which it leads.

Monotheism has primed us to see things in absolutes, in black vs. white, good vs. bad, in dualisms. This is not necessarily the way things are. These two things---restoring our ancestral traditions and living a modern life---are not, in fact mutually exclusive, but it speaks volumes that so many folks seem to think they are. As I tell my students: things were not always so. Our world is as it now stands because of choices made by individuals over the course of a generation. We can make different choices. Things do not have to be this way in the future.

So, think about where your ancestors come from. Think

about the traditions that they practiced for generations upon generations before the insurgence of monotheism, before monotheistic conquest, before what several friends and fellow ancestor workers call the monotheistic occupation. Think about what was lost and how in ways large and small, we can begin to get it back. This is ancestor work too and it's crucial. I say over and over again, it's going to take both sides of the equation living and dead to right the imbalance of our world and to restore our severed traditions and each one of us has an important part to play in that.

Tip: It's often good to cleanse before approaching any shrine. In my House we often use variations of lustral water and asperse face, head, and hands. Here is one of my favorite recipes (though really, water in which burning bay leaves have been extinguished would suffice). In a large pitcher, combine the following:

1/2 cup lavender water
1/2 cup rose water
fill the rest of the pitcher up with good, clean regular water
add a teaspoon of white kaolin clay
a handful of kosher salt
a tablespoon of jasmine flowers (I used dried)
1/4 tsp of cinnamon
a dash of High John the Conqueror oil

Chapter 3

"Walking, I am listening to a deeper way. Suddenly all my ancestors are behind me. Be still, they say. Watch and listen. you are the result of the love of thousands."

(Linda Hogan, Native American writer)

With this chapter, we're going to get to the meat of ancestor work technology. I have a friend who refers to it that way: as tech. All of these things that we're learning to do were part of our polytheistic ancestors' technology for engaging properly with the Gods and spirits. They formed a system of practice, of *protocols* that enabled people to effectively and *safely* engage with the Powers. It was all tried and true over many, many generations and I'm willing to bet stories of the occasional poor dumb schmuck who thought he could get results A, B, and C without going through the necessary techniques and protocols were passed around the campfire more than once, along with the unfortunate results of such experiments. These technologies still work too. That's the really amazing thing. They're right there for us to tap into and utilize in whatever ways are most appropriate in our lives.

Before I go on, I want to share something that I wrote earlier this year on my blog. It's a little anecdote that my colleague R.S. sent me in an email. Now I usually don't care at all about popular culture and I watch very little television but I'm really wishing that I had seen this particular show (though I suspect she summed up the best part right here). There was a powerful piece of ancestor wisdom in it---much to my shock. I mean, one just doesn't expect to find substance or ancestor wisdom on *NCIS: Los Angeles*!

Anyway R.S. told me that in a certain episode ("Kill House") there was the following scene, and boy does it ping with verity (as she also commented).

To quote her directly:

"The scene begins with the two senior agents walking Nell, a very intelligent young woman who is being trained for field work after distinguishing herself in the operations center, through the crime scene. She is nervous. They ask her if she feels up to the assignment. She asks how do you know if you are ready/up for something (I forgot the exact words). They said you trust your training, then tell the following story (again, I forgot the exact wording)....

24

"One year, Hetty (played by Linda Hunt), brought in a Headhunter for their field training. He was a real Headhunter, descended from a Headhunter who was, himself, descended from a Headhunter. He was taught the art of war-craft by his Father who was taught by his Father who was taught by his Father, and all down the line. The techniques the Headhunter taught them had been proven effective by each generation of his family who used them. When he drew his weapon, 10 thousand hands drew his weapon with him.

"This 'pinged' True--we draw upon the inherited experiences of our Ancestors."

That is it precisely. None of us walk alone. Wherever we go, we go with a retinue of our ancestors at our back. When I bow before my altar, my entire lineage all the way back to the beginning bows with me. To connect rightly and properly with one's dead, to engage them well and consistently is to know that when you act, ten thousand hands and hearts, minds and wills act in tandem with you. That is the power of ancestor veneration.

Something that just hit me now, retelling this: when you honor your dead with awareness and commitment, you're helping your ancestors honor their ancestors too, you're taking part in a spiritual cycle going back to the beginning of human evolution and probably farther (we don't know anything about the spiritual life of non-human beings on this earth). That's something terribly profound.

One of the most fundamental and in my mind best techniques and practices of which I know is that of setting up an ancestor altar or shrine. Just like with the Gods, it's often very useful to give yourself a visual and kinesthetic representation of the welcome that you're extending to your ancestors in your life. The ancestor shrine stands as a space marker, a sign to the dead that "This is your space. I'm giving you a place in my life. Be welcome." Now in actuality, we are all ancestor shrines walking. We carry our ancestors and our lineages and our helping spirits with us but even so, as creatures of Midgard (the human world) it's very helpful to have a space in your home or apartment or living quarters set aside specifically for your dead. It's a really good focal point. It makes a powerful statement to our dead.

The question inevitably is "What constitutes a shrine?" Well, it really depends. I have an entire credenza for my ancestors. It's in my dining room and it's the space they specifically indicated they wanted. I also have a separate altar for my adopted mom whom I honor not only as my mom but as a Heathen *sancta*. I've known people to make their ancestor altar a grouping of photos on the wall with a small shelf where they could light a candle and put out an offering glass. I've known people who lived in very, very cramped circumstances to decorate a pretty box, and keep photos and such inside the box. They'd open it up, light incense, pray, talk to their dead, make offerings and then close it all up again. I've known someone who kept a prayer book that had belonged to her great grandmother. She decorated the book and kept her photos and mementos inside. I've known people who've used bookshelves, or who set up three-dimensional artistic sculptures. Ancient Romans would have a nook by the front door where every morning the family would honor their ancestors and the household spirits. Part of that shrine were death masks of their ancestors. I would give my eye teeth to have a mask of my adopted mom.

I was talking to a friend once and I mentioned the Victorian custom of making hair jewelry out of the hair of deceased loved ones. You find elaborate brooches containing hair and pictures, artwork all made of hair, watch chains, necklaces, bracelets, hair ornaments, etc. Sometimes they did the same thing with teeth. She was utterly creeped out and found it "disgusting" and I have to wonder why. It's a powerful memento of a loved one. I for instance have my mother's ashes worked into a memorial tattoo on my back but I'd still love to have something that I could hold and look at when I'm thinking of her. How do we grieve and more importantly, how do we reintegrate the dead person into our devotional lives, into our memories, into our waking moments? These are questions I inevitably take to my ancestor shrine.

Making a shrine is a very personal thing. No one can tell you that your shrine is wrong. It should reflect the relationship that you have with your dead just like a personal altar reflects your spirituality and relationship with the Powers. There are a couple of caveats of course. Keep it clean and active. Don't let dust accrue. You wouldn't allow the room of an honored guest to become foul, so don't allow your ancestor space to become so. Don't put living people's photos on the altar (we've already discussed that), and try to be consistent in your practice. Ten minutes talking to your dead over a cup of coffee each morning is better and more effective, in my mind, than an hour once a week. As a friend of mine said: don't be that relative that only calls when you want bail money. Keep up good relations with your dead people.

Now for many years I had a roommate who was a Lukumi practitioner and I first learned how to set up an ancestor shrine from him. When I knew it was time for me to get serious about honoring my dead, I asked for his help because that particular tradition has a serious focus on ancestor work. He taught me how to make what is called a 'boveda.' (This actually comes from 'espiritismo'— spiritualism---not Lukumi, but it's found its way into the religion.) My ancestors took to this, so my own basic ancestor altar has a very Lukumi-ish flavor. I didn't realize what a mark it had left until I was teaching a workshop on ancestor work at a seminary, and I laid what's called a 'white altar' (white cloth, flowers, etc.) and five people, all having been raised in Cuban Lukumi households gathered round it with happy sighs about how it reminded them of their homes. This, of course, amused me greatly but if you're utterly confused about where to start, this might be helpful.

To make a boveda, set aside space---a table or windowsill or bookshelf. Cleanse it with Florida Water. Put a white cloth on it. Add pictures of your dead. Add a couple of glasses of water (the number varies from 1 to 9 depending on who is teaching you), add a candle and there you go. You may bring tobacco, flowers, or any other offerings you want. Spend time there each day. In spiritualism, at least as I was taught, and this holds true for many African traditions as well, white is a color of spiritual cleanliness, sort of the hazmat suit of the ancestor working world so if you're totally at a loss as to where to begin, you might try a boveda.

You don't have to do that though. If you're at a loss as to what to put on an ancestor altar and a boveda doesn't feel right, start with a pretty cloth, candles, and pictures of your dead if you have them. Then add things that remind you of your dead. If you have stuff that belonged to ancestors, pop that on there (you can put it in a box or on an offering plate). If you have things from the countries of origin of your ancestors put that on there. I have two Lithuanian dolls in traditional folk costume on my altar to represent my Lithuanian tribal mothers. It's been very effective. Hanging over my altar is a 16th century map of Basel, where not only my adopted mom came from, but my biological mother's ancestors also. Experiment and do what works for you and for them. You should have a sense of satisfaction when your altar is complete. Don't be afraid to change it though: altars and shrines change to reflect where we're at and in the case of an ancestor altar, where they're at too.

Several questions inevitably arise:

1. How long do I leave offerings out and what do I do with them?

This is probably the most common question that I get. The answer is: however long you and your ancestors want. Usually, though, I'll leave it out overnight and then discard it the next day. Sometimes, if I have to go out but want to make an offering, I'll just announce when I put it on the altar that I have to leave in such and such a time and at that time I'll be throwing the offering out. There's no hard and fast rule. I discard offerings as I would the remains of a meal for an honored guest. Usually I put them in the trash. Sometimes I throw them in the woods behind my house. It depends on several factors and if I ever have any questions, I'll divine.

2. Should I honor my monotheistic ancestors?

Yes. Honor your monotheistic ancestors (unless of course they were abusive to you, in which case—best case scenario-- an elevation might be in order). The exception to this, for me and some of my colleagues, is that generation which consciously chose, for whatever reason, to abandon their ancestral ways and embrace monotheism. Those we do not honor. Those we call out. We name their shame and confront them with it. We demand that they make reparation, that they work with us and with our other ancestors now to repair the damage to which their poor choice led. We're cleaning up their mess after all. The beauty of wyrd is that they are still able to affect it even after they are dead. They can make reparation and if they choose to take responsibility and do so, then they too may join in the veneration the other ancestors receive.

As to those who were raised monotheist and who may have been very devout in their own way, they bear no shame. Honor them just like you would any other ancestor. They'll let you know if they want something specific, or don't like a particular offering. Ancestor veneration is for everyone. We all have ancestors after all. Give them their due.

Besides, some of those monotheistic ancestors may have been parents, friends, and grandparents. They may have been people you loved dearly in life. That love doesn't go away just because they're dead. It's only right and proper to honor them.

In other words, honor them but don't emulate their mistakes.

3. What if I don't know their names?

Honor them anyway. Do a general call to your maternal and paternal lines. They know you. In time, information will come in the most random and surprising of ways. For now, just take those first faltering steps. If you're adopted, you have four sets of ancestors to call upon if you wish: biological maternal and paternal; adopted maternal and paternal. Adopted ancestors are your ancestors just as much as biological ones. My strongest ancestor is my adopted mother so I know something of which I speak here.

SUGGESTIONS

Set up an ancestor shrine.

Look for ways that you can do ancestor work daily. It might be little things, like stopping by a local graveyard on the way home from work, or donating to your dead mother's favorite charity, or telling a story, or comforting someone who is grieving. It may even be smaller things than that but keep your eyes open.

Consider writing a prayer that you can use to begin your ancestor work. It can be as elaborate or as simple as you like. Mine tends to start with a prayer of thanks to the Gods and ancestors and then I name my ancestors asking for blessings on them, e.g., "Linnie Hanna (my grandmother), may she be blessed." Finally I close with a prayer that they nourish me and keep away sickness, misfortune, and harm. Play with this and see what works for you. Sometimes 'set' prayers are a useful foundation from which to begin a practice.

Chapter 4

"It is good to act on behalf of posterity."

(The Teaching for Merikare)

This chapter addresses the top ten questions that I tend to get about ancestor work. I'm culling some of this from an article that I wrote a couple of years ago, because those questions haven't changed. Neither have my answers. Some of these are very basic, but you'd be surprised how the most basic of questions can come up as a stumbling block toward developing practice. So without further ado here you go.

Question 1: If I offer tobacco, do I have to smoke it?

This question always makes me laugh. It's a good question, but being a now and again smoker, I have vivid memories of an incident that happened to me about fifteen years ago. I walked in on my Santerian roommate trying to make an offering to Ellegua. He was trying to smoke a cigar as part of his offering. He was also green, coughing, hacking, and all but doubled over. The poor boy was not a smoker. I just took the cigar and smoked it for Ellegua and later, when everything was over, and the ritual concluded, laughed my head off. Of course after that, I was also the one smoking those cigars every Monday for my friend's weekly Ellegua ritual---no good deed goes unpunished after all!

To answer this question, however: no, you do not have to smoke the cigarettes you give as offerings. In fact, I usually don't. I might smoke like a chimney when I'm doing ancestor work (tobacco consecrates in a very special way and renders that which is said sacred; for some of us, we were taught to keep it lit usually by smoking our own cigarettes during ancestor work), but when I give tobacco to the ancestors, I almost never smoke their offerings. You can lay out loose tobacco too or just the loose cigarettes. If you're leaving the cigarettes in a public place (say at a grave) take the filters off first. Discard the filters in the nearest trash can. They aren't quite so biodegradable as the tobacco itself. I also recommend using American Spirit tobacco, as it is very pure. The tobacco offerings on your altars can be thrown in the trash after a day or so.

Question 2: What do I do with the offerings?

Well, my usual answer is: it depends. Usually I set out food and other offerings and leave it sitting out for at least twenty four hours. After that, I take it outside and put it either in the woods behind my house, or for liquid offerings, I pour them out at the base of a tree in my garden (a very happy tree that must be drunk as a skunk most of the time given how many offerings I make!).

Sometimes, particularly with ancestors who lived through the Depression, specific dead will object to food being left out for them. In this case, invite them to eat with you and share your own meal with them. Don't leave it out, but as you eat, make the meal and offering of time and attention, a family dinner, with your dead.

For the most part, the majority of ancestors seem to like food offerings though. I usually, with the exception noted above, tell people not to eat food that's given to the dead. It's theirs. You wouldn't want someone eating off your plate after all. When the time comes to discard, if you're able, put it outside, but if not, simply throw it in the trash. Be respectful, of course, but understand there's no onus on having to discard used up offerings in the garbage can. Deal with it the way you would the remains of a dinner party. That's my rule of thumb.

Question 3:Why do you knock when calling on your ancestors? (This came about after I posted descriptions of House Sankofa rituals which often begin with us knocking either with our hands or with a special staff on the floor.)

This is something that many of us have picked up from African and Afro-Caribbean traditions. It is a reminder to us and acknowledgment to them that they are our roots, that this is not about being in the head of over-intellectualization; it's about a connection that is deeply rooted in our very DNA. It's in our gut, in the blood, pain, struggle, piss and shit of living. It is a reminder to get down and honor those roots.

Question 4: How would you go about honoring ancestors when you have no connection to their culture or their God(s)?

This can be a real sticking point in developing an engaged ancestor practice. It's so much easier to honor those ancestors with whom we feel some measure of connection, after all. So firstly, don't beat yourself up because you don't feel a connection with a particular set of dead people. It's normal. It happens. Sometimes it may be that ongoing work is required to access that line. If that's the case, you'll find out as you grow more deeply into your ancestor practices. I would simply include that particular line in my offerings. Even if you feel nothing, thank them and make the proper offerings. It will benefit you in the long run and may actually help heal and strengthen that line so you can access it. Basically: fake it till you make it is a good rule of thumb.

Beyond that, cook traditional meals that are associated either with those specific dead or with their culture. Cooking is a very powerful means of connection and mutual nourishment. Listen to the music of those cultures. If you're very brave, learn the language of your ancestors. Learn their dances. Incorporate these things in whatever way you can into your practices. These are the things that sustain and create traditions and a great deal of wisdom and knowledge is bound up with them.

Also, read fairy tales and folk tales of whatever culture your ancestors embodied. If you want, and you have the means in your local community, become involved with the appropriate cultural societies. Often such groups hold local events and it can be a good way to get your feet wet with learning about your culture. There's also usually food involved.

Question 5: If one feels no connection whatsoever to blood ancestors, how does one go about creating a relationship?

The first thing I usually suggest---as you know---is to set up an ancestral altar or shrine and begin engaging with them by way of offerings. It doesn't have to be elaborate: a glass of water, a candle, maybe some flowers, and most of all your time and attention. Talk to them. Ask them to be part of your life and look after you. Thank them. You have ancestors stretching back to the very beginning of human life, to the moment the first amphibian crawled out of the primordial muck and decided to give land living a try. If the most recent generations of your blood ancestors are unhealthy or hurtful for you, go further back. Go as far back as you have to go. You don't need to know their names either in order to honor them. They all know you. They are connected to you by an endless line of births and deaths, of experience, of hopes, dreams, and struggles. Honor that. Good or bad, you're here because of them.

Doing things 'right,' by the way, is very subjective. There's no one way to go about this, really. There's engaging deeply and consistently and all that might entail. Each person is going to develop their own unique way of doing things, because in the end, our ancestors will guide us in this process as much as anything we read and they are individuals with their own likes, dislikes, opinions, and personalities.

Most of all, be patient. It took me over ten years to develop a really strong, engaged ancestor practice. It was hard and sometimes frustrating work until one day it clicked. Now it's one of the most rewarding aspects of my spiritual life. Just be patient and keep at it.

Question 6: What happens when your ancestors are from a different religion (usually Christians, but they could even be atheists) than you are? Could you honor them the same way? Do they want to be honored by another religion's rites?

I've only rarely found this to be a problem, and then there were other issues impacting the relationship as well. In the majority of cases, it's not an issue. Honoring the dead need not include calling on any specific Deities. It's a process of engaging with your ancestors and that's a relationship, you're not in that alone. They have ways of making their wishes heard. Even if all your ancestors were Pagan, it's likely they might have been devotees of different Gods and Goddesses which can be every bit as complicated as having a house full of monotheists.

I would say honor them and be open to allowing them to guide the process. I have a grandmother who had a deep relationship with the Virgin Mary. So, one day I was getting pushed very, very hard to buy a statue of Mary. Now I'm Heathen. I don't have any type of relationship with Mary but I bought the statue. It arrived and I had it tucked under my arm and was walking around my house wondering why on earth I bought it and I crossed in front of my ancestor altar. Immediately I knew. I looked at my grandma's picture and went 'YOU!' Well, the upshot of this is that she now has a Mary statue next to her photo on my altar. I don't honor Mary at all, but she did in life and I guess that's something she wanted in death too. Another ancestor pulled the same thing with Ganesh. I just go with it. It's their altar/space after all and you're honoring the connection, their influence, their support not their Gods. They can decorate their place however they want.

Question 7: What if the ancestors that come when you call aren't really ancestors? Instead they seem to be ancestors of type—the connection is through a tradition or behavior and chosen affiliation rather than strictly by biology. Do blood relations or chosen relations 'count' more as ancestors?

It's not all that unusual to have unrelated 'ancestors' become part of your ancestral house. Some indigenous traditions actually have specific names for the various types of ancestors: blood vs. affinity. Besides, friends, teachers, and mentors who have died can and should also be honored as respected ancestors. I don't think that one is more important than the other. If we go far enough back, we all share common ancestry and I think it's good and proper to honor them all, regardless of whether the association is one of blood, adoption, or affinity. Usually one or two of your ancestors will step forward to maintain and organize your ancestral house. They can be depended upon to keep things in order and can be petitioned for advice or aid if you're confused about what to do.

There are also heroic ancestors, those who were keepers of their line, or who did heroic deeds in life, or who, for some other reason, are above the norm, even cultural heroes (like Cú Chulainn amongst the Celts, or Achilles to the Hellenics) who might call for offerings and inclusion. For those of us who are priests, diviners, healers, shamans, mystics, warriors, craftsmen, etc.--any profession really--it's also important to honor your lineage ancestors. If you practice a craft, for instance, you are the most recent in a long, long line of men and women who strove for excellence in that same craft. They can help you. They're what I call 'lineage' ancestors. As a shaman, for instance, I am part of a lineage stretching back into pre-history. It's like having been adopted into a really large family. They should be honored too. Those of my direct lineage (the teachers of my teacher, etc.) within that require special attention. If you feel particularly strange about it, you can always give them their own special space on your ancestor altar.

It's part of ancestor work: sometimes you'll acquire ancestors. When I first visited a local cemetery, I had a couple dead folks want to come home with me. The first time I went to a Civil War cemetery, one of the soldiers and I developed a certain affinity and now he is honored with the rest of my dead. I have a colleague who made a grave rubbing of a Colonial Era grave and the lady whose grave it was followed him home. Now he has to hail her as an ancestress. Sometimes your own ancestors might bring other spirits in. I once encountered a lonely spirit hovering wistfully outside my house after a major ancestor rite. I took offerings out to him and said that if my own dead agreed, he could come and partake of the ancestral offerings that I lay out. That's just the way it works. Dedicated ancestor workers tend to encounter this an awful lot.

Question 8: How about what do you do when your ancestors don't want you to honor them, or otherwise do not respond or show interest in your devotion?

In twenty years, I've encountered this three times. Each time, there was a very good reason for it. Before I gave up on honoring them though, I would try to seek out a good diviner or ancestor worker to see if I could find out why. It may be that something needs to happen or be done first and if that's the case such guidance can be invaluable toward righting one's ancestral house. There may be legitimate reasons though for the lack of contact and a diviner or ancestor worker can help you get to the bottom of the matter so at least you know what's really going on and can act accordingly.

Question 9: I have, after much careful consideration, decided not to have children. I have the clear impression this is displeasing to them. Given that my decision is non-negotiable, how can I establish a good relationship with them when I am refusing to continue to very bloodline that connects them to me? I would be very grateful for any insight you can offer.

Well, it's important to point out that there is no hard and fast rule to ancestor veneration other than 'do it.' When you deal with your ancestors, while in some respects it may seem as though you're dealing with a monolithic unit, in reality, you're dealing with individuals. It may be an organized counsel of individuals, a collective, but in the end, you're engaging with a conglomeration of individual people.

While it is meet and right to respect and honor our dead, that doesn't mean that we are bound to obey their every dictate. Working with the ancestors is a process of engagement, *negotiation*, and mutual reciprocity. There's wiggle room there in most cases. Sometimes, they will push very hard. Sometimes we do too. Part of ancestor work is negotiating space where your needs and theirs can co-exist. It's perfectly okay to have certain hard lines with them. If not having children is your hard line (and it's mine as well, by the way) then the thing to do is to sit down with them. Hold a personal ancestor ritual, call upon them and explain this. Tell them that you will honor them. You will welcome their strength and protection and wisdom into your life, but---and this is non-negotiable---you will not have children. You will share their wisdom with those who come into your life, with those you care for, but they will have to look to other parts of your living line for children. They can push---doesn't hurt to ask after all---but you are not obligated to comply and this is where maybe seeking out a skilled ancestor worker and having that person negotiate and facilitate the conversation can be very helpful.

Not having children in no way means you can't have a deep and engaged ancestor practice. You may find it's one or two ancestors who are fixated on this because it's one of the ways that they define health and well-being. This is workable. If you have siblings who do plan to have children, point this out. Direct them there. If not, simply state your position and continue to engage. Call upon other ancestors to help or seek out a capable ancestor worker to sort things out. Usually, as with any relationship, ongoing communication is the key.

Question 10: What is an ancestor? Can you define the term exactly?

We've already covered this in Chapter 1, but it really is one of the most common questions that I get so I'll answer it again here just for good measure. I use ancestor as something of a catch-all term. It certainly applies first and foremost to those connected to us in some way by blood and/or adoption. It also, however, may be applied to those connected to us by lineage or affinity. The elemental Powers are our ancestors: fire, water, the mountains, ice, wind, trees, stones...they have their own medicine that they can share with us if they wish and predated us by millennia. The Gods may be considered ancestors in some traditions....it's a very nebulous term if you get right down to it. I usually think of it as 'dead people and those from whom they descend' with the unspoken understanding that it is those who have a place in my spiritual house. Here's the thing though: they have to be dead. This means that they existed. Your ancestors are not fictional characters and they're not metaphors.

There's one other question, really a corollary to the

above, which I'm going to throw out here because in the next chapter we start learning what to do to heal tangled, damaged, and destructive ancestral lines. This goes beyond the question of how you honor ancestors with whom you had a complicated and not always good relationship in life. Rather, it's what do you do with ancestors whose actions in life (for instance, like being instrumental in genocide) are actions that you completely disavow. Moreover, what do you do when some of your ancestors were the victims of atrocity, and the others were those who perpetrated those self-same atrocities? Light stuff, right? What do you do when one of your ancestors committed atrocities on others of your ancestors? This is something every person of color in the U.S. descended from African slaves has to face. This is something almost every Native American has to face. This is something all of us from European lines also have to face. What if part of your line were Spanish conquistadors and the other part the indigenous peoples who were conquered (read raped, tortured, enslaved)? What do you do if part of your line is Jewish and part German and you know you had committed Nazis in your line? These issues don't go away. They are carried down the ancestral lines just like the horror and damage these things caused don't just disappear from our society because we wish it so. There are numerous ways to address this in ancestor work and there are ways to bring healing to your ancestors, to restore broken lines. It's not easy. It's horribly painful and it's something we're going to be discussing next. For now, I wanted to give you some preliminary thoughts.

These questions are so involved and so very complex even to an ancestor worker like myself that I actually called my colleague, a woman without a doubt the most gifted ancestor worker I know, for a consult! We hashed out what we would advise in such a situation and that's the advice that I'm going to give here, but in truth there's no easy, pat answer. I don't know what I would do really, until I was faced with that situation and did the necessary divination (or, if I weren't a diviner, sought out someone to do so for me) and prayed to my Gods and Disir (ancestral guardians, powerful female ancestors) for guidance. Still, this might give you a working game plan, should you find yourself in this situation with no one nearby to consult.

A. What if I had a really bad relationship with an ancestor in life?

This is actually the easiest of the questions to answer. It's really not all that uncommon a thing. It's important to remember that relationships can continue to grow and evolve and even heal after a relative's death. In a situation where the relationship in life was unhealthy or hurtful, you have a couple of options. You can call upon your other ancestors to help you repair the relationship or you can begin a series of elevations to help heal that ancestor.

It might take time, but it is possible to work through a great deal of hurt and anger and to turn such a relationship into a strong ancestral bond. There has to be willingness on both sides, though. If the living relationship was so abusive and so hurtful that even contemplating an elevation is a horror, then there is no need to do so. You can always appeal to older, stronger ancestors, to your Disir, to the guardians of your ancestral line (we all have dead who take this role) to keep that person away. What you do depends on the nature of the relationship and its history. There is no one answer here.

B. What about ancestors who committed atrocities, like genocide?

There's a big difference between dealing with an ancestor who may have been personally hurtful in life, or who may have been an asshole (we all have those people in our lines somewhere), and dealing with an ancestor who was a sociopath, a war criminal, the willing participant in genocide or someone who committed a massacre, or who might have been a serial killer, etc. What do you do then?

I have to admit, this question really left me at a loss. It's one that I knew I'd have to address sooner or later, but I'd been trying to make sure it was 'later' rather than now. Still, people are asking and it deserves an answer. What do you do if, for instance, your grandfather was Josef Mengele?

I'll share my colleague's advice first:

"Most people would do exceedingly well to leave a sociopathic ancestor alone. Or, if that ancestor starts making trouble, appeal to some stronger members of one's ancestral house to keep the deviant one effectively sidelined. I personally would not honor such an ancestor. Now, if you want to be Machiavellian, and you are someone who engages in some rougher forms of magic, you might be of a mindset that this is potentially an ancestor who would be willing to do some very dirty things to your enemies for payment. That is a possibility, though I wouldn't suggest it personally. It could very easily come back to bite you."

I tend to agree with my colleague: healing an ancestor and developing a relationship with an ancestor has to be reciprocal. Unless I were pushed to do so by my other ancestors (or the Gods), I very likely would not honor such a person, or attempt to engage with them in any way. Some traditions even have specific rituals to bind such spirits away from one's ancestral house. Moreover, courting such an ancestor in the hopes of having a willing servant is not only dangerous, but also stupid. It has the potential to lead to one being attacked by that ancestor and then fed upon and possibly even corrupted by the lich. By inviting them to do your dirty work, you would also have made yourself lawful prey outside of the protection of your other dead.

If I were pushed to engage for some reason by my other ancestors, I would only do so under their direct supervision and protection. It is possible to heal and restore a line, and it's not impossible for such an ancestor to come to a point of wanting to make reparation but it would take some convincing for me from other, reputable members of my line before I'd go there. Says my colleague, "If trusted ancestors give you the push or your Gods do, I'd listen. The ancestor in question may be trying to clean up the family wyrd and make amends. If so, I believe we should help. If they are willing to work to fix it."

C. What about when one part of your line committed atrocities on the other?

This too, sadly, is not so uncommon, especially in the U.S. Some of you may wonder what exactly I mean in the way I phrased this question. Well, perhaps you have a lot of Native American blood, and also the blood of one of the military men who committed their careers to exterminating them. Perhaps you have the blood of Nazi officers and the blood of Jewish victims. Maybe you share Hutu and Tutsi ancestors. Perhaps you have Native American blood from two different tribes: one that fought the European invaders and one that collaborated. Perhaps you have the blood of African slaves and the blood of slave owners....do you see where I'm going with this? Those conflicts don't just miraculously evaporate once everyone directly involved is dead.

You may be called, as part of your ancestor work, to engage with both sides of this ancestral equation and it very likely won't be easy. Here's what my colleague had to say:

> "Most people who have ancestors from the African Diaspora also carry some European blood, specifically the blood of slave-owners and rapists. I have this in my own family tree. I also have Native American blood and European blood, which carries with it its own history of genocide. How I deal with it is like this: I do not have an issue with the Europeans in my tree who did not commit genocide and who did not buy, own and rape my great-great grandmothers. I do not and will not honor or acknowledge those Spaniards who owned my foremothers. They get nothing from me. I call them out and say if you ever want me to give you a thing then you know the debt you owe, and the price is working to make things right, work to heal the damage that was done. Some ancestors are unrepentant and they are too toxic to touch and you may have to pick a side if there are branches that cannot be reconciled."

You may find the same dynamic occurring if one of your ancestors was an abused spouse and the other the abuser, or an abused child and the abusive parent. In fact, you may find that in order to begin untangling these threads and bringing some measure of healing to your lines, you may be forced to go back very, very far, to some of your oldest ancestors and get them involved. It's okay to call upon other ancestors for help with this. They have a vested interest in getting things right. If the oppressor, abuser, attacker sincerely wants to make reparation, you'll have an easier time of it, but note that does not mean 'easy.'

Beyond that, just understand you're in for some hard work, work that won't go away just because you might decide to refuse to deal with it.

SUGGESTIONS

Go and visit a local cemetery. Introduce yourself to the dead. Make offerings. Be respectful. If something needs tending/cleaning, do it. Write in your journal about this experience.

Chapter 5

"The most disastrous aspect of colonization which you are the most reluctant to release from your mind is their colonization of the image of God."

(Dr. Frances Cress-Welsing)

This chapter might be a rough one for some folks. If this is the case, if you find yourself becoming emotional as you work through it, that's okay. That is an expected and even appropriate response. Give yourself the space to experience whatever this brings up. Now it might not and that's okay too regardless of how it falls out, but I want folks to know that this is a potentially intense chapter. Sit with it. Meditate on it. Let it do what it's going to do. See how your dead respond also.

Sometimes our ancestors were really fucked up.

There's no getting around that. We can excuse it by relativizing the cultural and ethical expectations by virtue of the time in which they lived (not something I myself necessarily do, but I've seen it as a coping mechanism); we can sometimes avoid those ancestors; we can pray for them, elevate them (which we'll be learning in this lesson), and a dozen other things to cope with this when it occurs on the individual level. It's a bit more painful and problematic when it occurs on a group level, a community level, a large scale level. That's not quite so easily dealt with and yet, at a certain point in our work, this is precisely the level at which we are expected to engage.

I've found this isn't something that one must necessarily seek out. Sooner or later, for many ancestor workers, those consistently doing this work will stumble upon these things themselves. It can happen with individual ancestors---you'll discover an area of intergenerational pain and wounding that needs to be addressed---or one gets dumped into one of the two great wounds of our collective lineage. The only good thing about this latter is that it's not yours to heal alone; we're all responsible for engaging with this process in whatever way we can. We each have our portion of this to shoulder. Sometimes, I will admit, this is cold comfort.

So before going farther, I want to be quite clear about what I mean by "two collective wounds." In restoring our ancient polytheisms, in honoring our ancestors, those of us who are polytheists are attempting to reclaim and restore our indigenous religions. Those reading this who may not be polytheists are attempting to get right with their ancestors so they can live a better, healthier, more fulfilling, more prosperous life. Either way, this can come up: there are two ancestral wounds with which we must contend.

1. The destruction of our own ancestral traditions.

The spread of monotheism across Europe was, by the original definition, religious and to some degree cultural genocide. It did not happen smoothly as a history defined by the Christian victor would like us to think. Conversion was one of ongoing bloodshed and conflict. It was a matter of conquest, often politically fueled (though just as often if not more often religiously motivated) and it resulted in the destruction of our traditions, quite often by outright force, equally often by implicit force. When we talk about reclaiming our traditions, restoring the indigenous lens through which our ancestors viewed the world, one question follows hard on the heels of that goal: what happened to those traditions? Why don't we have them? Where did they do? The answer to that is simple: monotheistic conquest.

(As an aside, some of you may notice that you have trouble not immediately thinking 'Native American' or 'First Nations' when you hear the word indigenous and this is not uncommon. The thing is, everyone comes from somewhere. Think back to what John Trudell said in his "Tribes of Europe:" at some point we all had tribes. What soil holds the bones of your dead? Where were your grandparents and great- grandparents and great-great-grandparents born? Go back seven, nine, twelve generations. Where are your dead buried? We all come from somewhere. We are all indigenous---which means native, as in 'born at/of ---to some place. Christianity in general (since that is largely what Western Europe dealt with) and monotheism in particular is not indigenous to Europe or Africa. It is a mutation of a Mediterranean cult that at one point was nothing more than a radical Jewish sect. (I highly recommend Reza Aslan's book on the life of Jesus, *Zealot: The Life and Times of Jesus of Nazareth*, by the way, for anyone who wants to get a sense of the political, economic, and cultural narratives surrounding the life of the historical Jesus. It's a fascinating read.)

Monotheistic religion is not what our ancestors, prior to about 1500 years ago, practiced. It was a set of traditions largely forced upon them.

There were, as we've already noted, those who willingly converted, those who---for whatever reason---willingly and often doggedly abandoned their ancestral ways. Care must, I think, be taken to distinguish the person who did so happily and of his or her own volition and those who were forced compelled, and threatened into it. Think, for instance of how the Orkneys were forcibly converted: the men go out hunting and fishing; Danish troops come into the village, round up the women and children; the men come back and everyone is given a choice: convert or we kill your family. That is a horrific choice. That is a choice no one should *ever* have to make under any circumstances. I don't hold those ancestors culpable for the destruction of our ways. In fact, there is archaeological evidence that in the northlands, many of our ancestors buried sacred relics and Deity images, godpoles and the like to keep them safe from profaning hands and from destruction during the period of forced conversion.

To touch directly upon the experiences of the ancestors that lived through this---or did not live through it actually---to experience them directly as some can in ancestor work (for really strong ancestor workers, if you have the right combination of gifts, your dead can share their experiences, emotions, sensations, memories with you directly; it can be painful and traumatic when those memories and experiences surround something of this magnitude but, if they can endure it, we can stand witness) is an intensely wrenching experience. It changes everything. What you see what was truly lost, experience in your bones the effect it had on the wyrd, on our world, on your own lineages, nothing is *ever* the same again.

2. The second wound with which those of us of European ancestry must contend is what happened after that.

In some sick and twisted form of cultural Stockholm syndrome, our ancestors ate the poison of their conquerors. They came across the ocean, they went into Africa and did to other people what had been done to them. They became the destroyer of nations. There is a tremendous debt there and it's one that we inherit whether we like it or not. Ancestral debt doesn't just go away. If it is unaddressed, unacknowledged, unexamined, and unhealed, it comes down in the line dogging each generation. It's not, after all, as though the consequences of conquest aren't with us every day. This shit hasn't stopped. It may not be happening now with weapons and outright violence, but it's happening. It's enshrined in the very fabric of our dominant culture. Conquest doesn't just affect one generation. It has long lasting and damning results.

Nor is this just a European problem, an American problem, an African problem, et al. It's a human problem. Period. The balance of our world will not be addressed and righted until all sides of this equation are working together to bring healing.

One of the things that I have found very powerful, is paying cultus to mitochondrial Eve. This is the African woman from roughly 200,000 years ago who is the common matrilineal descendant pretty much of us all. (This is no joke. For instance, I went to genebase.com, one of several human genome projects that will run your DNA. I can trace my maternal line back to Senegal, to the second migration of Eve's descendants, who left Africa, went through Greece and Turkey, up to Finland, and down into Germany, Switzerland, etc., etc.). She predates the filter. She has the medicine to render us immune to it. She has the medicine to help restore our world. She is, I believe, rather seriously pissed too. She and her daughters, our eldest tribal mothers are calling for honor, calling for cultus. Paying cultus to her is an excellent way to stab the filter in its eye and start the long, slow, painful process of healing. The rest, I find will come as one's own ancestors bring to light the individual work that one is best able to do on this front. It will be different for everyone. Not giving yourself a pass on issues of race and privilege are a good start, because racism is one of the most devastating effects of conquest. The video "The Pathology of Privilege" by Tim Wise (youtube.com/

watch?v=YN8pmhQwcnY) is brilliant. It's an uncomfortable topic but one that it benefits us to address because this shit, if you'll pardon my being blunt, will eventually arise during the course of deeply integrative ancestor work.

Now, there is a way to help damaged ancestors. It's a ritual called an 'elevation.' This is a ritual that can be done over the span of nine days to help elevate and heal troubled ancestors. It is designed for individual ancestors. There are no small acts in working with the dead. Healing one ancestor contributes to healing these great and grievous wounds. It is possible to take on the process of contributing more directly to their healing, but that is something that your ancestors will guide you in---how that is best approached is different for everyone.

A ritual to elevate the troubled dead

Ancestor elevation is a sacred practice that is done to help the soul of a dead family member who was troubled or angry or depressed in life, perhaps doing harmful things to themselves or others, perhaps never able to live a happy life due to their own inner demons. By doing this, we aid their souls in finding peace. It is an act of mercy, and can also be an act of emotional freedom for the living, especially if their own lives were negatively affected by that individual when they were alive. It is ironically a lot easier to do this work for someone after they are dead. Unlike the act of simply wiping them from one's life, this practice actually helps the problem at its root.

Begin by laying an altar on the floor. This is done in part because the ancestors are our roots, and in part because during the course of this nine day ritual, we will symbolically be raising the altar and thus lifting our ancestor up. Be sure to place this somewhere where it can remain out for nine consecutive days. If you have pets, that's okay. It's not going to harm anything to have them drinking out of offering glasses.

The altar should be white: white cloth, flowers, candles. Culturally for us, this color still speaks of faith, purity, and spiritual cleanliness. In doing an elevation for a particular ancestor, we are engaging in ancestral healing, in cleansing a tiny bit of mess, blockage, pain, strain, hurt from that particular line. White, representing cleanliness to us, is a good color to use for this.

Set up a picture of the dead person you wish to elevate centrally on the altar. (If you don't have a photo, write their name on a piece of white paper in your best handwriting.) It should be noted that an elevation can be done for a beloved ancestor just because you love that ancestor and want the best for him or her. While they are usually done in the case of troubled, aggressive, unhappy, unhealthy ancestors or conditions, they don't need to be reserved only for those cases. The only pre-requisite to doing an elevation is that you must already have a primary ancestral altar and an engaged ancestral practice.

Put out flowers. Prepare a candle, a glass of good, clean, fresh water, incense, and whatever other offerings you wish to make.

When you are ready to begin your ritual, set a candle at each of the four corners of the altar and light them, offering a prayer that fire will cleanse and consecrate this space, making it sacred, making it a place where clear communication may occur between you, the ancestors, and the Holy Powers. Call upon any God or Goddess Whose help you might wish in this endeavor. Ancestral work is a very personal thing. It not only involves us and our spiritual connections but specific ancestors and their spiritual connections. Regardless of the fact that we are Heathen, Norse Pagan, or Northern Tradition, etc., we may find ourselves called to put representations of Deities our ancestors honored on the altar, or to call upon Them. This is not about us. If you have a grandmother who had a close connection to the Virgin Mary, and in the course of an elevation, you get a sense that you should put an image of the Virgin on the altar, I'd suggest doing it because really, who is better positioned to help elevate that grandmother than the God or Goddess who Whom she prayed her entire life? Get over yourselves, people.

Sit in front of the altar (on the floor) and call to the

ancestor you are elevating. Light incense, and the main ancestral candle. Begin by offering the following two prayers on behalf of this ancestor (these are the ones I commonly use, but feel free to use others if you wish):

First Prayer:

Hail to the Gods and Goddesses.
Your grace illumines all things.
Your gifts shine forth,
Making fruitful nine mighty worlds.
Blessed are those that serve You.
Blessed are those that seek You out.

Holy Powers, Makers of all things,
Bless and protect us in Your mercy.
Lead us along the twisting pathways of our wyrd
And when it is time, guide us safely along the Hel-road.

Second Prayer:

(This prayer was originally written by Fuensanta Arismendi for the Gods she loved above all others, Loki and Sigyn, but you can readily adapt it to your own devotional connections)

My Lord and My Lady, my Beloved Ones,
May those you call always hear Your voice.
May I always love You beyond trust and mistrust.
May my surrender be complete and voluntary.
Give me this day the grace of Your presence.
When I fail You of Your kindness,
Permit me to make amends.
Use me and teach me according to Your will,
And deliver me from all complacency.

Third Prayer:

Call directly to the ancestor you are elevating and say:

Oh clement and merciful Gods,

Magnificent Holy Powers hear my prayer.
I offer these prayers for the soul of X,
And for all good spirits who wish our prayers and recognition.
Please let X know that someone here on Midgard
Is stepping forth to speak for him/her.

Merciful Holy Powers,
And all other good spirits and ancestors
Who might intercede for the relief of this soul:
Grant him/her hope.
Grant him/her the awareness
That he/she is illuminated by the Divine light,
That he/she is younger kin to the Gods,
Beloved of the Holy Powers.
Let him/her see those tangles in the wyrd,
Those hurts and imperfections
Which keep him/her away from peaceful tenure in the realms of Hel,
From rebirth, from renewal.
Open his/her heart to understanding,
Grieving, repentance and restoration.
Let him/her understand that by his/her own efforts
He/she can make the time of his/her testing easier.
Wyrd unfolds always, and living or dead
The power to weave it well is in our hands.
May the Holy Powers and other helpful ancestors
Give him/her the strength to persevere in all good resolution,
To meet the tests of his/her wyrd rightly and well.
May these benevolent and loving words
Mitigate and soothe his/her pain.
May they give him/her a demonstration
That someone in Midgard acknowledges, remembers
And takes part in his/her sorrows.
May X know that we wish him/her happiness.

At this point, offer the glass of water to X. Put X's picture and the glass of water on a book (cover it with a pretty cloth so it's aesthetically pleasing). Remain meditating and praying for as long as you wish. When you are ready to end the ritual, you may leave the candle to burn for a bit, or blow it out. Thank the elemental power of fire for holding and consecrating the space as you blow out the four corner candles. Thank the Gods and ancestors and then your ritual is over.

Repeat this for nine consecutive nights. Each night, clean, fresh water should be offered and the water and picture lifted by the addition of a new book. After the ninth day, the picture and offering glass of water can be placed on top of the main ancestral altar.

A caveat: if the candle or the glass breaks, you should do three things:

> Start the entire elevation over.
> Call upon your disir, and other strong and protective ancestors to guide and watch over the ritual.
> Put pieces of camphor in the water. (In traditional folk magic, and in spiritualism from which the concept of elevations originally evolved, camphor is protective. It keeps destructive spirits away). If you want to use a more traditional Northern herb, sprinkle dried agrimony. If the altar is very active, change the camphor or agrimony every day and do not use the candle. Usually your strongest ancestors will come forward to help with the elevations anyway.

I have found that the dead like to be remembered with food, drink, offerings but also with music. It would not be inappropriate to offer music during this ritual. At the end of the whole thing, when the elevation is complete, it is always good to make an offering to all your ancestors, and to make an offering to the Gods upon whom you called for help.

You may do elevations for the same ancestor multiple times. It does not hurt. In fact, with particularly damaged or angry ancestors, or tangled wyrd, you may have to. It's not a bad gift to give a beloved and healthy ancestor, though.

This is something that I initially learned within the Lukumi tradition but it's a very flexible ritual. Take it. Adapt it for your own use---I did. Use whatever prayers you're comfortable with. The symbolism of the rite is very clear: you are raising the ancestor up. You can also (and should) call on your other ancestors, your helpful and strong ancestors to assist with the elevation. This is important, as is praying before you begin each night because sometimes ancestors who need elevations, even when they want it, will fight and resist. Sometimes it can be hard work. I would suggest cleansing yourself before and after you do your nightly elevation, if you're working with a problematic ancestor.

It sounds like a simple ritual, but it's not. Put your whole heart and will into it. You are literally raising your ancestor up and that means by extension you are raising yourself up. I have seen someone go through initiation, or go through the process of elevation and have it be so incredibly powerful that it brought healing not only to hir, but to the entire line ---both ancestors and other living descendants. Elevation is a powerful, powerful thing when it's done well.

We each have our ancestors and that's a good thing and we work with them individually. But at some point 'ancestor' becomes a collective, because we are all interconnected and that collective stands together as a powerful force. Healing one single ancestor, one tiny part of the universal human lineage, *your* lineage, brings healing and strength to the collective (of which we will one day be part) and that in turn renews and strengthens us.

SUGGESTIONS

If you can find a DVD called "The Language You Cry In," I highly recommend watching it. It highlights the power of ancestral connections even through depredation, slavery, and horror.

A Prayer for All Indigenous Peoples

(and all those struggling to reclaim their indigeny,
all those struggling to throw off the yoke of conquest.)

Hold strong,
May your ancestors sustain you.

Hold strong,
May you never bow your head in this fight.

Hold strong against these people,
who come with their foreign Gods, foreign ways
and no ancestral voices to speak for them.

The enemy comes offering bread.
The enemy comes offering books.
The enemy comes clothed in compassion
so that you will not see the poison behind their gifts.
That poison will destroy you.

Resist it with everything you have.
Resist it for your ancestors.
Resist it in the name of your Gods.
Resist it in the name of your people,
for your children,
so that they will have a future
in which their bellies and their spirits
will be fully nourished.

Hold fast, hold strong.
You are not alone in this fight.

Remember the sacrifices of your ancestors.
Remember the power and beauty of your people.

Do not allow the poison peddlers to divide you.
Engage, engage, engage
with all that nourishes you.

Drawn upon the wisdom and strength of your ancestors
And don't ever let it go.

May you be nourished in all that you need.
May you ever hold fast.

(I learned recently that the new ideological position of
Christian missionaries is that, as a colleague of mine wrote:
"The un-G-O-D-ed folk of the world are now being referred
to as 'unengaged,' not just 'unreached.'" We both wonder
when this new position was taken and what it means to them.
We also continue to take deep umbrage at that
narrowly-focused target that gets placed on the backs of the
world's otherwise *quite* fully and functionally 'engaged'
indigenous people. We are not unengaged. We're unbrain-
washed. There's a difference).

A Note on Indigeny

I have talked and written about reclaiming our indigeny
extensively over the past couple of years. It's crucial toward
the reclamation of our ancestral traditions because restoring
those traditions is not just a matter of returning to the
worship of specific Gods or doing specific rituals but of
rooting ourselves in the understanding, the *Weltan-
schauung*, the way of looking at the world, and moreover the
way of interacting with the world integral to many if not all
indigenous ways. I'm going to step back for a moment and
discuss the concept of indigeny, what it is, what it means, and
why it is such an important touchstone. Of course, I'm
probably going to ramble a bit and maybe wander off on a
tangent or two so prepare yourselves.

The world was not always predominantly monotheist. In
fact, monotheism is a very new and very young interloper in
the world of religious identity. There was a time, not too
long ago, when not only was Christianity not the dominant
religion in our corner of the globe, but the dominant
religious fabric of society---pretty much *all* societies---was
defined by honoring the ancestors, maintaining their
traditions, and making proper offerings to the Gods and
Goddesses of one's people, region, land, family, and personal
devotional life.[1] The dominant way of looking at the world
was one deeply rooted in this diversity of religious thought.

It was, in other words, polytheistic.

I find (and here's one of those tangents I was warning you about) that when people ask my religion, which happens occasionally since I work at a seminary, and I respond that I am polytheistic, there is often a moment of cognitive disconnect in the questioner. It's as if the word does not compute. Inevitably, upwards of ninety percent of the time, their response, after thinking about it dumbly for a few minutes is to ask "but you believe in Jesus, right?" I believe in all Gods and I tell people so, I just worship a select few of which Jesus is not One. In fact, from my perspective one would argue whether or not Jesus is a God or elevated ancestor, not that it makes much difference in the long run. This of course often causes more confusion. Why is polytheism so difficult to comprehend for the average monotheist? I believe the answer to that question lies in the fact that it is an open-ended system, one rooted in tradition but welcoming of diversity of thought and approach....an attitude dramatically and diametrically opposed to that of monotheism. Basically, we're using spiritual muscles the average monotheist doesn't have, and we're doing it without nice, pat little answers like the promise of salvation to help us. It's not that they can't connect the dots. The average monotheist, to put it bluntly, doesn't even see all of the dots. They're blinded by their own religious filter, one rooted not in the ways of the ancestors, but in the doctrine of discovery, in conquest, colonialism, and brutal destruction in the name of one divine power. But as I said, I digress.

Indigeny is what came before all that.

The words 'indigenous,' 'indigeny,' or, to use the proper academic term 'indigeneity' all stem from a Latin word *indigena, ae*: native, born in (a particular area).[2] This in turn hearkens back to an earlier Greek root which means 'to be or to become.' It does not, as I have heard many a bigot disparage, bear any etymological relationship to 'indigent,' which comes from another Latin root (*indigeo, indigere, indigui,*) meaning 'to be in need.'[3] Thus when I speak about our indigenous traditions, I am speaking about our ancestral, native traditions. I am speaking about what our ancestors did long before the subjugation of Christianity. I am speaking about our religious traditions that evolved out of our relationships with our own native land and Gods and people. I am speaking about that cultural and religious sensibility that determined how we viewed every aspect of our world and which our ancestors took with them wherever they went, even if that meant relocating to a new land. Everybody has that, or had at some point in their lineage's history. Everybody.

When I talk about Heathenry, or Hellenismos, or Celtic Polytheism, or Kemetic Religion, or any other Polytheistic faith, essentially I am talking about those beliefs and practices, traditions, and ways of engaging with the world that existed in a specific place before monotheism tried to wipe them out. They evolved within a specific cultural language. I'm talking about what our various ancestors did before they were forced to convert. These are our traditions, our birthright. For this reason, I do not believe and will adamantly argue with anyone who claims that these contemporary polytheistic religions are 'New Age.' They are not new age. They are not, in fact, new. They are restorations, informed by modernity of course, but hearkening back---granted, more than a little imperfectly in some cases---to the traditions of our ancestors. Were it not for the aberration of monotheism and the endless conquest to wipe us out of existence, our traditions would not be in need of restoration.

Of course authentic, and---a word I use quite a bit because it seems to fittingly descriptive of what's necessary to do this process well---engaged reconstruction is a difficult thing. It involves the long, hard, slow, and incredibly challenging process of breaking and chipping away at the filter of monotheistic conquest with which we've *all* been raised.[4] That's not just difficult, it can be terrifying. After all, we have no direct experience of anything else. If we remove that filter what will replace it?

The difficulties go beyond even that, however. The best way that I know of to begin that process of reclamation, to begin rooting oneself in one's indigenous traditions, to begin challenging and removing the post-conquest filter is to connect to and maintain a relationship with one's ancestors. This is the ultimate power of ancestor veneration. It provides a means of self-definition when that unhealthy filter falls. Our ancestors lived the very traditions we're trying to reconstruct after all; who better to inspire and guide us in reconstructing them?

In connecting with our honored dead, however, one is brought face to face with certain issues. For those of us coming from European ancestry, two specific issues tend to arise and they are painful ones. Firstly, when one talks about reclaiming one's indigenous traditions it begs the oh-so-salient question of why? What happened to our indigenous traditions? Where did they go? Why don't we have them now? One of the first stumbling blocks one faces in connecting to the ancestors and reclaiming one's indigenous mindset is facing the fact that our ancestral traditions were destroyed by the long term religious genocide that was the spread of Christianity across Europe.

Lest you think my use of the term 'genocide' egregious, allow me to point out that the man who actually coined the term in 1944, Raphael Lemkin, specifically noted that genocide need not mean the immediate destruction of a people or a nation. Instead, it included a "coordinated plan of different actions aiming at the destruction of essential foundations of the life of national groups, with the aim of annihilating the groups themselves [even if all individuals within the dissolved group physically survive]."[5] Lemkin specifically notes calculated destruction of a given people's religious practices as indicative of genocide. Under this rubric, the United States government's forcible removal of Native American children from their families and their subsequent incarceration in government run schools wherein they were forcibly Christianized in an attempt to destroy Native cultures could be classed as genocide.[6] So too could the Christianization of Europe.[7]

This leads me to the second horror one must eventually face. First we have to face and deal with what was done to us and our traditions; then we have to look at what that turned us into. First our own traditions were destroyed and then, in some mad form of cultural Stockholm syndrome, we became the destroyer. We turned around, perfected the techniques of conquest and came across the ocean to do unto others what had been done, five hundred years before to us. As difficult as this may be to look at, it's essential that we do so. If our ancestors could undergo these things and perpetrate them, the least we can do is look at them cleanly and squarely. It is the first and perhaps the most necessary step toward reclamation: to be able to look at our own history good and bad squarely in its proverbial face and without flinching.

Does this mean we shouldn't honor our recent ancestors, ancestors who likely were monotheist? Of course not. None of us are perfect. If your ancestors were, for the most part, good people, honor them; that doesn't mean you have to perpetuate their mistakes. It doesn't actually mean they have to perpetuate their mistakes either. After all, that is the beauty of wyrd: even after death, through the channel of ancestor veneration we are able to empower our ancestors to continue working in the world and many, upon being reunited with their kin, more than realize their mistakes. The destruction of our indigenous ways did not occur overnight or without resistance; neither will their restoration.

I have said it before and I shall say it again: it's going to take both sides of the equation living and dead to right this wrong. It's going to take both sides working in tandem to restore our broken, damaged, lost traditions. It can be done though. In this, I have utter faith. Christianity sprang out of nowhere. It came from the death of one man and the machinations of his followers vying for power. In a very short period of time it came to dominate the globe. Our traditions do not spring from nothing. They do not depend on any one person. They grow from roots sunk deep into the consciousness of our ancestors. It only takes connecting to those ancestors to give them the chance to live again. This is our sacred obligation if we're going to call ourselves polytheists. The key to restoration isn't found in faulty lore. It's not found in donning the garb of peoples past. It's not found in super-imposing modern prejudices over ancient beliefs. It's found in the long, hard work of connecting to the dead and learning to see through their eyes, learning to engage with the Holy Powers with their sense of piety. It's found in our indigeny and reclaiming it.

We as a people need desperately to return to our pre-Conquest mind. What Conquest is it that I'm talking about? I am talking about the conquest of northern Europe by monotheism. I am talking about the destruction of our ancestral religions, the severing of our ancestral connections, the corruption of our tribal cultures. I am talking about genocide. I think ideally, as we work to restore our traditions, we should be focused on reclaiming our sense of our own indigeny. It can be beneficial to talk and network with other indigenous peoples. Not to co-opt their Gods; we have our own Gods. Not to steal their ceremonies; once we've restored our connections, our ceremonies will come. But to learn to see and relate to the world once more through indigenous eyes. This was our birthright. Unless ET dropped you off on a fly by, this is your birthright too. If we go far enough back, every last one of us came from a tribe, from an indigenous tribal tradition. That includes those of us of European stock. It's about time we remembered that.

Reclaiming our indigeny means learning to engage with the world in a completely different way. It means learning to engage with the ancestors, the land, and our Gods in different ways too. We've all been taught, first with the corruption of monotheism, and then with the Protestant Reformation and later the 'Enlightenment' with its deification of science, to avoid connection, and to look upon our ancestral ways as something primitive. In reality, the ancestors, Gods, and spirits of the land are our connection to all that is. We are the container of our ancestral line. We are its living manifestation. We're an expression of life on the earth. We're connected to everything that is. Why are we pretending otherwise? Why are we allowing the system, the filter of Conquest to dominate our reconstruction, to poison it from the very beginning.

We've all been taught to filter religion through what can be known by external sources, external authorities like

62

written texts. The spiritual world of our ancestors was far different and, in my opinion, far richer. In reality we need to look at the framework of every other indigenous religion on the planet. The commonalities are there: knowledge comes not from books, but from the connection with our ancestors and with our Gods and with the land itself. Instead of reclaiming that precious structure and mindset of indigeny, we've replaced that structure with something very alien: monotheism, greed, fear, and disconnection. Instead of looking at how other people have preserved their ways, we are asking Snorri Sturluson, a man who was a Christian and therefore a man who had an agenda. One wonders if the stories as Snorri recounted them bear any resemblance at all to the tales our ancestors would have held as sacred. We as Heathens need to take a good, long look at the way our ancestors did things. These are not people of the book. If they were, you'd have stuff written by them. They were people of action, and of connection. They were connected to place, to their ancestors, to their Gods. They had not been raised with this falsehood that the Gods want nothing to do with us. They knew they were intimately connected their Holy Powers.

Thankfully, we can still have access to that connection. That line has not been broken. It is held by our ancestors. Do not let the machine, the contagion that flows from monotheism cage your mind because until you learn to think differently, to remove the filter that most of us barely realize is there, there's been no conversion, no reclamation. There's just substitution and we all might as well be Lutherans. I think our ancestors are calling us to wake up. Restoring our tradition is an experiential process. It's about forging that sacred connection and from that connection everything else can be rebuilt. From that connection, from active engagement with our Powers, everything else can and will flow. It's not about standing solemnly in a circle, not about the rite or content of the rite itself. All rites whether you are Lakota, Yoruba, Hellenic, Roman, Norse, or even Saxon are to facilitate one thing, not to avoid or substitute, to facilitate direct connection to the spiritual powers that nourish us:

ancestors, Gods, and land. Long ago, in order for us to be conquered that connection had to be amputated. In order to be conquered, we had to be taught to look for that connection in books or outside ourselves rather than in the dirt where our ancestors' bones are buried. You think you're not indigenous? Where are the bones of your people? What earth contains them? You come from a place. You come from a people. You come from a line. You come from a tribe, from something that is so much bigger and you want to trade it away for lore, lore not even written by people who practiced their ancestral traditions? From lore written by collaborators? That lore is not designed to bring you to any reality or connection. It is a product of the corporate machine. It's a product of soul sickness and spirit sadness. We have eaten the poison of our conquerors and in some sad sort of Stockholm syndrome, we continue to deny ourselves the only antidote that matters: ancestral connection, connections with our Gods, direct experience, and a reclamation of our own indigeny. In other words, our birthright. It's time we all wake up.

Notes

[1] This is true even with the growing rise of Monism in the ancient world.

[2] See *Chambers Dictionary of Etymology*, p. 521, entry on 'indigenous' and *Cassell's Latin Dictionary*, p. 300, entry on 'indigena, ae.'

[3] See *Chambers*, entry for 'indigent,' p. 521.

[4] Even if one was raised non-religious, in America our society is strongly impacted by Protestantism in general and fundamentalist Protestantisms in particular and the social, historical and, until recently, the political fabric of Europe was also dominated by Christian values.

[5] Quoted in *A Little Matter of Genocide* by Ward Churchill (p. 70), this is part of the original definition of genocide as found in Lemkin's book *Axis Rule in Occupied Europe: Laws of Occupation, Analysis of Government, Proposals for Redress* (p. 92).

[6]Not to mention the actual calculated disenfranchisement and slaughter of thousands upon thousands of Native men, women, and children throughout the history of European dominance of the Americas. For this reason, during the UN summit on genocide in the late forties, America used its influence to have the definition of genocide watered down to the point that it is effectively meaningless....where indigenous cultures are concerned.

[7]This mass conversion, often forced, had its share of bloodshed.

Chapter 6

"Hear me, ancient ones, you who have dwelt in this place for the ages. You are blessed among the assembled. You are remembered. You have reached the time of the returning, of the in-dwelling. May your hearts be lightened, may your livers be joyous. The remembering comes. Eat dust no longer, venerated ones, but join us at our tables. Eat with us. Lend us your wisdom. Let us be one people again. May we find restoration together. Let it be done."

(Tess Dawson)

Preparing a meal is one of the most fundamental forms of nourishing and caring for someone. It strikes at the heart of what a Tantrika friend of mine would term 'root chakra issues:' survival, safety, engaging with the body. There is something very primally pure and powerful in preparing a meal and sharing it with loved ones. It is the most essential means of support. This holds true for ancestor veneration as well. One of the best things you can do for your dead is to hold the occasional ancestral feast.

I suspect, though I've not had this independently corroborated, that part of the reason for this is that so much of a family's folklore is stored in its kitchen. In feng shui, the kitchen is the heart of the home and likewise I suspect that it's for just such a reason. If you want to learn about a family, cook with them. There is powerful knowledge passed down from grandmother to daughter to granddaughter and intergenerational. Stories and recipes, family hexis, a means of behaving and engaging with one's family community---all of these things are learned via osmosis, via observation and engagement through the act of nourishing a household. The folklore of the family begins in the kitchen. For this reason, I often tell people who are beginning to honor their dead and who want more solid ways to connect to their lineages, to cook the foods that were traditional in their families (no matter if it's just simple rice and beans, or pot pie, or whatever---cook what was shared at your household table). If you didn't have that experience growing up, cook the foods common to your ancestral ethnicities. Just like learning a loved one's language, cooking foods they like, foods that remind them of their parents, and would remind those parents of their parents, etc., is a powerful means of fostering connection. Food is sacred. It's also magic.

In many indigenous religious traditions do you know who the most important person in the whole ritual is? It's the person handling and preparing the food. In hoodoo, an American synthesis of African, European, and Native American folk magic practices, food is crucial. Many of the most powerful charms are worked through one's food. This is true of both healing and hexing. There have even been studies done wherein scientists postulate that what makes us human, what prompted our own evolution into what we know as 'humanity' was learning to cook. Working with fire and working with food actually changed the way our brains work. Food is the building block of community and conscious civilization.

A huge part of how we engage with our ancestors involves food: we make offerings. We pray and give them water. We talk to them and give them a bit of food. While some ancestors (usually those who lived through grievous famine or the Depression) may fret if a descendant gives food and may not want it, the majority of ancestors respond tremendously well to the gift of food and drink. (In the case of ancestors who fret, share your own meal with them. Invite them to eat with you, or find out what they will accept.) Sharing food and drink is crucial.

It's also easy to expand this into special offerings of a full ancestral feast. Many Pagan denominations do this at Samhain or Winternights, holding what is termed a 'Dumb Supper,' a silent feast where the ancestors are given their due. As a friend of mine likes to say: "don't be the relative that only calls when he needs bail money." In other words, don't go all out just once a year. Every so often, at important birthdays and death days, for special occasions, or just because you want to do something nice for them, prepare an ancestral feast.

What does this entail? Well, cook for them (or if you're really hopeless at cooking, go and buy the food from a local restaurant, though *learning* how to cook, even if only simple things, is a fantastic offering in and of itself). Lay out a feast, or at least a nice meal. Let them have it all (you may even get the sense, as I sometimes do, that they're talking and hanging out amongst themselves as they 'eat'). The next day, dispose of the meal however you wish---we've already discussed options in a previous chapter. I sometimes even take this to local graveyards. There I might stay and read for a couple of hours and then clean everything up and leave, or I make sure my offerings are biodegradable (no tin pie pans for instance) and leave it well concealed (one graveyard has a bit of forest behind it, another has a hollow tree that has seen many an offering and not just from me, etc.). Liquids can be poured out, flowers left without raising questions. Tobacco after dinner is also an excellent gift (you don't have to smoke it). This is really adaptable technology.

SUGGESTIONS

Make a feast, a really nice dinner for your ancestors.

Write in your journal about how this goes.

Learn a few recipes from one of your ancestral lands.

(If it's an interest for you, learning an ancestral language is also an amazing way to connect to them, even if you just learn a few polite phrases).

As a tangential to this chapter, I also want to bring up the ideas of miasma and taboo.

Heathenry doesn't talk much about miasma but I'll bet our ancestors knew what it was. The Romans and the Greeks surely did. It is spiritual contamination. Now this does not in any way imply sin. It does not imply any wrong-doing (though wrong-doing can bring one into a state of miasma too). At its base level, it means that person came into contact with a thing or situation that rendered them no longer spiritually and/or energetically clean.

While honoring the ancestors doesn't put one in a state of miasma, coming into contact with a dead body does. Visiting a cemetery might. (Weddings do too, by the way.) This is a normal part of living a good and healthy life. Miasma can also occur when one is in the presence of something foul, impious, or unclean. The solution is to ritually cleanse before engaging with the sacred. So when I do my cemetery visits, I cleanse before I go (usually just by aspersing myself with Florida Water or khernips---a Greco-Roman means of purifying where bay is lit on fire and doused in water, rendering the water sacred) and I change

70

my clothes and cleanse when I return. I might also cleanse at least symbolically by washing face and hands before engaging with my dead. The reasons are two-fold: when in a state of miasma, our signal clarity isn't as good as it could be. Also, excessive miasma can attract negative things. I'm sure there are more reasons too, but those are the two that I worry about the most! Cleansing before and after work will help, as will cleansing regularly energetically. This is part of good devotional practice.

Sometimes---not always but sometimes---people get hit with taboos when they start this work. For instance, I must salute whenever I pass a cemetery. I use a Yoruban gesture representing the Orisha of the Cemeteries. Another ancestor worker will kiss two fingers and hold them up; another bows and offers a very brief prayer; another, former military, actually salutes. We find what works. Sometimes, in exchange for the flow of blessings, quite often to foster the flow of blessings, ancestors will give you taboos. It is a means of harnessing power. It is a mark of respect, a gesture of commitment. Sometimes those taboos will be rigidly enforced (as in break them and you'll get puking sick as well as being in miasma) and sometimes they're guidelines that you are expected but not compelled to follow, guidelines that ultimately will enhance your practice even if only by making you more mindful.

SUGGESTIONS

Think about taboo and miasma and, if you are so moved, journal about it.

If you can, get and read a copy of Robert Parker's *Miasma*, which explores the concept in ancient Greek religion. Mary Douglas also wrote *Purity and Danger*, which analyzes pollution taboos in the ancient world. I recommend both.

Chapter 7

"Divination, then, more than any other religious act, confirms not only that the gods exist, but that they pay attention to us."

(Sarah Iles Johnston)

Throughout this book I've been trying to emphasize that the dead are the protection of the living. They are there for you and will help sustain you. You do not need to be a medium or have any special facility for communicating with them. You will both find a way if the consistent work and desire to do so is present (which it is in all of you). Now, while you don't need to be either a master diviner or a medium, it does sometimes help to have a means to check communication. I mean, let's face it, sometimes we all experiences times where our 'signal clarity' is off. Strong emotion can do it, exhaustion, stress, illness....any number of things. Sometimes I think what psychic sensitivities we do have close off in the face of really strong or excessive input. I've certainly had that happen. It's a safety mechanism.

There are any number of divination methods that you can use to communicate with your dead. Because teaching extensive and involved systems of divination is beyond the scope of this course, I've decided to teach you a simple, binary system: Hermes coin divination. It's good, no matter what other systems of divination you know, to have a binary system in your tool-kit. One, it has the advantage of giving you clear yes/no answers. Two, it forces you to craft your questions very, very carefully and with as little ambiguity as possible---because if you're at the point where you need to do this, you're probably worried about filtering things accurately. A clear yes/no is a godsend. Because I learned this system from Sannion, for lineage's sake, I asked him to teach it to you all here. So the following part of this lesson is from him. (Thank you, Sannion!)

Sannion's Lesson

Hermes was connected with all sorts of humble forms of divination in antiquity. According to the 4th *Homeric Hymn* Apollo would not grant his brother a share of Delphi's famed oracular prophecy, but instead gave him the bee-maidens "who know how to speak the truth" to divine with, and Zeus commanded that "glorious Hermes should be lord over all birds of omen and grim-eyed lions, and boars with gleaming tusks, and over dogs and all flocks that the wide earth

74

nourishes" (568a-573) whose movements could predict the future if men were inclined to learn the art of interpretation from him. Hermes was also sought to grant prophetic dreams (Odyssey 7.137), presided over divination by knuckle-bones, dice, or pebbles (Apollodoros 3.115) and *kledones* or omens derived from overheard conversations. (Pausanias 7.22.2).

In keeping with this spirit, modern Hellenic polytheists have come up with a very simple form of divination which is especially appropriate for Hermes since he is also the god of commerce and the inventor of money (Suidas s.v. Hermes). While it is fairly primitive and can't expound on the complexities of a given situation, it can be quite helpful in a pinch, especially when you need decisive answers. And when used properly you can actually manage to tease out a good deal of information from it.

Basically, the system works like this. First you should pray to Hermes in your customary manner and ask him to grant you insight on the given issue. You may either choose to speak your question aloud or do so silently, as I haven't noticed a difference one way or the other. Then take out three coins. Ideally they should all be of the same value, so that each factor is given equal importance, but if you only have mixed coins in your pocket that will do. Three coins is best, that way your answer won't come out a stale-mate as might happen with four, an otherwise preferred Hermetic number, and you will also have enough information to consider the question properly. Using only one coin limits the effectiveness of the oracle, although in a pinch that works too.

Toss the coins and note how they land.

> Three heads indicates a definitive YES.
> Three tails indicates a definitive NO.
> Two heads and one tail indicates a generally favorable outcome, though there may be some minor conflict involved; there may also be some contingency you're not aware of and should look into more; or consent is only grudgingly offered, and

while it will likely come about, it perhaps should not.
  ➢ Two tails and one head indicates a generally unfavorable outcome, one which has a chance of being salvaged though it will require a great deal of effort to do so; too little is known about a situation to provide a definitive answer; you should examine your motives and see why you're still clinging to this hope even when you know that it won't be.

There are other ways that you can interpret the fall of coins, especially in the context of your question, and as with most forms of divination you should allow your intuition to guide you.

This form can be very useful when you are trying to gain a diagnostic understanding of things. One question can lead into others as you pare down all of the probabilities. However, as with all forms of divination, once you have received a clear answer you should stop asking, as to continue is considered very bad form and potentially insulting to the divinity.

It is also important to understand when to consult the oracle. It's okay to use it when faced with a situation where you cannot possibly determine which of two options is the best, or when you are trying to ascertain information you have no other way of obtaining, or you need a quick goad to spur your thoughts into motion. However, when you already know what the outcome is going to be, or you are using it as a crutch so that you don't ever have to make a decision for yourself---then you have a problem. It is also important to understand that the information you receive holds true only for yourself. If you want to know what another person is thinking just come out and ask them! Don't try to weasel your way into their thoughts or hold them accountable for what comes out during the oracle. If you do that Hermes just might lead you astray in order to prove a point.

Although you can use any change in your pocket for this---especially if you're on the fly and in need of quick assistance---I've found that reserving three coins for special use as your divinatory tool can be very effective, especially if these coins are of foreign extraction, since Hermes is the god of travelers. If you use such a miscellany of coins it's okay if they don't all have the same face value, provided they do have both a discernible head and tail.

After you have finished your consultation you should thank Hermes for his guidance, and abide by what comes out. If you continuously disregard his advice he will eventually stop offering it. (End of Sannion's lesson.)

I would note that this system can be adapted with a set of coins being given solely to the ancestors, if one had no relationship with Hermes. I would also caution against over-use of divination. While divination is a sacred art, and it's absolutely right and proper to seek out guidance this way, and clarity, it is also possible to depend too much on it, and for it to become a crutch, separating you from clear communication with your dead, and stopping you from developing any sense of discernment. It's sometimes a fine line. The times I find this type of divination *most* helpful is after an offering has been made, or when contemplating one. You can call upon Hermes and ask for His guidance and then call upon your ancestors and ask them if they want offering X or if offering X was acceptable to them.

Some people have a dedicated set of Tarot cards that they use only for their ancestors and some use a Spanish Gypsy system called the 'baraja.' Any system I suspect could be used this way (I tend to use baraja or coins when I need extra clarification), though I would suggest having one set of whatever you're using consecrated and reserved solely for communicating with your ancestors.

There is no shame in seeking out a specialist. That is what we're here for. If you're encountering something with your ancestors, or are perceiving tangles and issues in your ancestral lines and threads and you have tried everything you know, and you're getting pushed from other ancestors, or just feel overwhelmed and scared and /or at a loss, by all means call in a spiritworker or shaman. I do recommend having a consultation/reading with a specialist at least once a year, but no more than every three months (again, too easy to get addicted to the process). It helps clarify issues that you may not be picking up on (it's hard to hit everything when you're in the middle of it!), and can also forestall any serious issues arising. I do this myself, seeking out one of my colleagues and vice versa in many cases.

One thing I really want to emphasize here is that ancestor work is polyvalent. It's a very, very individual thing. You are dealing with individuals after all and different families have different wants, needs, and customs. Everything that I'm teaching you here is meant to be a guideline to get you started. Once you take these techniques and run with them, your own dead will be your best guide on what to give, and how to do it. These practices are meant to be adapted and shifted, and made your own. They're fluid. The best way to make sure that your 'signal clarity' with your dead stays strong is to maintain the relationship consistently and to keep yourself free of miasma. All the exercises that you've learned in this book---the centering and grounding, filtering/shielding, cleansings----are essential to this type of thing. They'll help maintain clean, clear signal clarity and that is essential.

When you're sitting down to do divination like this, I would first cleanse and call upon your ancestors for protection. I do this as a matter of course as a diviner. I have a whole ritual praxis that I go through before a client walks through my door and more than I do after. I set up special protections and wards, I cleanse myself, I make offerings to my ancestors and to fire (which is one of my allies) asking that they keep the place energetically clean and protect me and my home (now office---I stopped seeing clients in my home some time ago) from any miasma or negative spirits the client might be carrying with him/her. I was initially thinking that I'd have you work on developing the same sort of structure but it's not really necessary unless you're divining for others.

What I would suggest, is that you think about what type of structure you'd like (and it's a fluid thing; you're not locked into one thing forever and ever once you decide) to bracket your more formal engagements with your ancestors.

It can be a very, very helpful thing.

For intense, I will usually cleanse myself and the area with Florida Water or khernips, light candles, and then offer certain prayers to my ancestors. Then I lay out offerings and we just chat. It really varies, but I always have that light structure to fall back upon in the event that I'm having a day where I'm particularly frazzled. I have grown more mindful over the years of the transitions into and out of such reverent space and it's something that I encourage you all to pay attention to as you go. I cleanse to mark my transition into this space and blowing out the candles, offering a formal prayer and cleansing again precedes my passage back into regular, quotidian headspace too. Play with this and see what you come up with. See what works best for you.

A Personal Note

I am thinking of my adopted mom tonight. I found one of the travel journals that I kept the first time we went to Paris. I kept brief notes, not even vignettes really just the barest sketch of an experience to spur the memory. My mother was a memory keeper in so many ways and this particular passage made me recall that, and how her very presence in a place opened people up to true mindfulness about what is really important in a life, and the impact of a life well lived. Here's the passage....crude, but I was not writing for publication (I go on a bit about food; my mom was teaching me about wine at this point and an appreciation of gourmet cuisine---both cooking and eating it---was a joy shared between us).

Tonight we ate at Le Grand Vefour. It's located in the Palais Royale and while the Seine is my favorite place in Paris, the garden courtyard of Le Grand Vefour is quite likely my second favorite. The water spirits are so palpable here. I could feel them rippling and laughing underneath the dirt and I am no dowser! I could feel the water running beneath the earth and beneath my feet. It had lovely energy; and there were echoes of everything this place had ever been, and all the people who had walked there before.

The restaurant was a lot of show. The wine, a 2001 Savigny-les-Beaune Champs-Chevrey from Domaine Tollot-

Beaut was excellent. It was well balanced with the food, had punch but no dark, expanding depths - just a bit of bite. It was pleasant. The food (lamb and veal) was good but not exceptionally so. I had fresh black truffles on a potato salad as an appetizer and while I far preferred Taillevent's sautéed truffles, fresh rock salt atop them really enhanced the flavors. I liked the raw tuna (actually it was very lightly seared or I'm tasting the high quality salt) amuse bouche the best. Dessert was ok but what I really liked were the candied figs and kiwi squares brought [also] as an amuse bouche.

The service, especially one waiter was incredibly good. I barely had to raise my eyes and he was there. Here is what I recall most about that night, and it still stuns me how quickly an epicurean delight shifted into something sacred, a moment out of time. My mom had been to that restaurant many times as a child - her family often traveled to Paris when she was small and when they ate out, they brought her as well. It was one of the ways she learned to appreciate food, wine, fine dining, etc. Because she'd been there so many times as a child, she had fond memories of a very well known sommelier - he had been kind to her when she was small. She inquired about him to the head waiter and that was when everything changed.

The entire staff - and I mean the entire staff - thronged about her when she mentioned she knew the sommelier - Monsieur Enoch (may he be hailed). He'd made a difference in her life. He was kind to a lonely child. He'd apparently left a similar impression on the staff. It was as though we'd fallen through a crack in the shifting eddies of time. Even waiters too young to ever have known him came to our table to pay their respects. Suddenly there was a sense of lineage. In a restaurant like this, serving as a waiter is a profession and respected. There is strict training and a sense of lineage. When I say that everyone working in the restaurant came to pay their respects to Monsieur Enoch, I mean everyone. She was their intermediary through which they paid respects to their ancestor, to their lineage, to every person who had served in their positions, in that restaurant before them. It was beautiful. It touched my mother deeply too. I think at that moment she realized that she's a part of the history of these places too, that she has left ripples in the streams of wyrd, that like Monsieur Enoch, there are people and places better because of her. For me, I watched this ancestor reverence and could almost sense Monsieur Enoch's spirit present in that place. I realized how simply being a decent human being, showing kindness in unexpected places, ripples through generations. This man was kind to a lonely child and she remembered him fifty years later and because she remembered him she was able to bring those who followed in his footsteps into momentary communion with his memory as an honored ancestor. If that is not holy work I don't know what is.

On wine, vine, and land

I'm a bit of a wine snob. I was taught by my adopted mother, for whom wine was one of life's sweetest pleasures. She had a very discerning palate, and with her training, I developed a palate that, had I chosen to pursue it, would have enabled me to take a sommelier's training. This was one of the grace-notes of Midgard, a pleasure we both shared.

Until she came into my life I'd never liked wine. I hadn't been exposed to much and didn't realize that a palate is something that must be cultivated, and that as it was cultivated it would expand and perception would deepen and a whole new world of taste and flavor, aroma, and insight would open up. When I asked my mom to teach me about wine, she took to the task with a vengeance. Over the years that we were together, she gleefully exposed me to some of the best wines in the world. It was, at first, an uphill battle! I have a sweet tooth and at first, that carried over to a dismaying degree in my choice of wines. I found anything not cloyingly sweet too bitter. So she solved this by starting with the best dessert wine she knew and very slowly and very, very patiently, moving my palate away from the sweet. My taste for reds and whites opened up at different times. The latter came first and took about a year to develop. I can still remember with vivid clarity that day, many years ago, when my palate burst open to white wine. I was sitting in Tour D'Argent, overlooking Paris and drinking a glorious, absolutely glorious 1999 Puligny Montrachet. All of a sudden my taste buds were flooded with multiple notes of flavor. I remember losing myself in a complex, multi-layered

81

smokiness that seduced the tongue and nose, unlike anything I'd ever tasted before. To this day my favorite white wines are still the ones that are rich and smoky. It took another year and a half or so for my palate to open to red wines. That was less dramatic and while I know I was in Italy (probably Rome), drinking a lot of Amarone, I can't name the exact time or place of that particular epiphany. With the opening of my palate came a growing sense of the spirit of the vine as well and I began to develop an alliance with him. My explorations of wine were grounded not only in deep and deeply sensual delight but also immense respect.

So my mom took me to Switzerland once, wanting to show me all the places that had formed the warp and weft of her world, all the places she loved. We were traveling through a small village near Montreux and stopped for lunch. The restaurant wherein we were eating offered only local wines, grown within a few miles of where we sat. These wines are, for the most part, not distributed broadly and are sold only in the immediate areas. Before I could venture an opinion, my mom cautioned me against turning up my nose up at local varietals. She told me that the spirit, wisdom, and medicine of the land upon which we stood was contained in those wines. It was a distillation of the 'ashe' of the land spirit itself, and contained trace memories of everything that had ever happened in those places. It's a connection, on a very deep level, to the power of the land itself, a very particular plot of soil. It's a means, a very sacred and holy means of absorbing the power of that land spirit---freely given---into oneself. To taste the wine was to taste the land upon which it was grown. (She also had much to say about why a wine tastes better in its native locale than after it's been loaded with sulfites, agitated, and shipped to the U.S., but that's another tale in and of itself.)

She was right of course and the more I thought about it, the more I realized that this holds true for every bite of food or drop of drink we put into our mouths. For this reason if no other, homage should be given to the spirits of the land, the soil, the tilled earth, the mulch, the water table, and the entire ecosystem in which our nourishment was born. As the land is nourished so are we.

Think about that: as the land is nourished, so are we. Truly grasping that one simple truism changes everything. I know for me, it transformed to a great degree the way in which I interact with the earth. I became much more conscious of what I put into my mouth, where my food comes from, how my local farmers are treated, and the megalithic horror of Monsanto and all the destruction it brings (and not in the name of science either; hubris maybe, but not science). I found myself radicalizing on fronts that I had heretofore ignored as someone else's fight. Well it's not 'someone else's fight,' not unless I suddenly no longer require food to live.

It's not enough to say "I honor the earth." Tell me how. What exactly do you do? How does it translate into your everyday Midgard life? Because words are not enough.

My mother taught me that, a bird-boned firebrand, a small, delicate woman with an elegant Swiss accent, a streak of blue in her hair (for Loki---and, according to her, so no one would look at her and think she was without her edges) and a will that would put the mountains themselves to shame. She was a radical: in her devotion, in loving the Gods, and in the way that she adored the earth. That is my inheritance.

Chapter 8

"Our greatest responsibility is to be good ancestors."

(Jonas Salk)

There are layers upon layers to ancestor work: rituals of devotion, visiting and cleaning up graveyards, leaving offerings there, doing good works in the name of one's dead, donating to worthy charities, telling the stories of one's dead, and, in oh-so-many ways, reweaving those threads. This is something that, in some way, everyone can do. It's just a matter of finding out what works individually and what one's own dead desire. There's one aspect of ancestor work that even the best of us often neglect, though: honoring the Elemental Powers. When I sat down to compile this book on basic ancestor work, I promised myself that I would not neglect this aspect of it.

In Norse cosmology, creation sprang from a synergetic collision of the world of Ice and the world of Fire. From this 'big bang' the first proto being, a hermaphroditic giant named Ymir was created. From Ymir sprang the first ancestors of the Gods and things took off from there. Each of these worlds has its sacred beings---Gods, spirits and assorted kin---and the gifts of each in some way deeply impact and bless the smooth functioning of our world (imagine, for example, if we didn't have any means of working with fire; cooking, pottery, glass, industry, travel, warming our homes, light and electricity…we'd be without all of that and more). Ultimately, ice and fire are our eldest kin. Beltane, with its emphasis on fire, passion, and the richness of the land, seems to me to be the perfect time to turn one's attention to the elemental powers which shape, form, and sustain our world. These Powers hold tremendous wisdom and they are worthy of respect. Somewhere along the line, we've forgotten that and it is yet one more thread that we're tasked with restoring.

There is a popular animation series, *Avatar: the Last Airbender*, which is based around the concept of elemental nations: the fire nation, earth nation, water nation, and air nation. I like that taxonomy quite a bit and, though this is not what the series intended or how it uses these terms, I've often found myself applying that idea to the actual realms of the Elemental Powers. Conceiving of fire as a nation in and of itself, a sentient community, a culture has the potential to dramatically change our conception of fire itself and by extension the way in which we relate to this family of spirits. The same holds true for the other elements. I think that's important because amongst all of our traditions and contracts that have been devastated, desecrated, and destroyed by the forced spread of monotheism across Europe (and even before simply by people's greed and arrogance), perhaps no family of spirits has suffered as much as the Elemental Powers themselves. We abuse our world and we do it unthinkingly. We take far more than our portion. It is yet one more method of colonialism and genocide encouraged by the monotheistic idea that we are masters of all we see, the top of the food chain, superior to everything else in the universe. We have forgotten how to partner with these Powers. We have forgotten what it means to stand not as their superiors but as respectful equals or even their younger kin. There is no balance.

As an ancestor worker and shaman, I think it's critical that we re-learn a measure of respect. I strongly believe our Elemental Powers are angry---and they have every right to be. If we as a species think that we can conquer and dominate them without consequences, the recent earthquakes and tsunamis, mine collapses, and that magnificent South American sinkhole should be clear signs that we can't, and we may pay a terrible price for our hubris. The Elemental Powers are crying out for recognition and respect, just like our ancestors; and just like with our human ancestors we need to recognize and grieve for the harm we have done them and then we need to roll up our sleeves, make some offerings, and get down to the hard business of fixing it.

So as an ancestor worker, I honor the elemental powers. I encourage others to do so as well: plant trees, nourish the soil, feed the land, contribute to local bee-keepers. Go and pour out offerings to a local mountain spirit. Mountains are our memory keepers. Fight to keep destructive practices like fracking out of your area; perhaps consider donating to organizations devoted to protecting the environment like the Big Sur Trust, or Scenic Hudson. Recycle. Reweaving those threads doesn't start with the big, grand gestures. It happens little by little, small action and small commitment by small action and small commitment. It happens with all the simplicity and grace of planting a seed and having the fortitude to see it to flower.

This is ancestor work too, and in the state of our world, as devastation of our own making pours into the oceans, taints our land, and threatens our environment, it's pretty damned crucial.

I think Wiccans probably have it the easiest here because the typical Wiccan ritual involves an invocation to air, fire, water, and earth. That's good, but even that, drawn as it is from ceremonial magic, is far removed from what I'm referring to when I speak about honoring the Elemental Powers. I'm also aware that like ancestor work, this is a new concept to many of you (as it was to me not so long ago) so I'm going to step back and explain exactly what I mean when I talk about this type of elemental reverence.

The Elemental Powers are ancient. They are also older by far than humanity and quite sentient. I very much like the idea of referring to Elemental 'nations' precisely because in our lexicon that implies a culture, community, and sentient, independent beings working and abiding together. I believe that these Powers, like the Gods and the ancestors, have the ability to consciously choose to affect our world. I also think that they have been injured, attacked, and ravaged by our species. Likewise, I believe very strongly that part of doing effective ancestor work lies in restoring right relationship between ourselves, each one of us individually, and these Powers. Of course every person is going to have to decide for him or herself what precisely that entails.

I came to honor the Elemental Powers through my work with the ancestors. It was a logical extension and one some of my oldest ancestors pointed out to me. As a Heathen my cosmology tells me that ice and fire are responsible for life. That great collision of opposing forces birthed the worlds, including our human world. That makes them ancestors of a sort. I'll fully admit that personally, I don't much like 'nature.' I'm not an outdoorsy type person. I much prefer a nice air-conditioned home with good food, good wine, maybe a little television to camping, hiking and peeing in the woods. That being said, I may not like being out in nature but I respect the Powers that inhabit and form it; and I've learned over the years to honor them. It wasn't easy for me. I especially found it difficult to overcome my distaste for personal inconvenience. When it dawned on me that to truly honor these Powers, it wasn't enough to say prayers and pour out offerings; I had the moral obligation to make a few changes in my lifestyle as well (like starting to recycle, for instance), it was a huge personal comeuppance. It was a necessary one, but I can't say I was initially graceful about it. My understanding of what it means to honor my ancestors and honor the Elemental Powers has deepened over the years but I well remember how difficult a concept it was for me at first and sometimes with this aspect of reverence, I still balk.

I think that when dealing with any of the Powers it's important (very important) to remember that they don't necessarily give a rat's behind about our spiritual evolution. The universe is not here to help us evolve. It is here for its own sake and its own evolution. I think that we're very self-centered as a species (perhaps every species is) and much of the cultural concepts with which we've had to contend over the past two thousand years have only strengthened that particular tendency. Whether we want to or not, whether we realize it or not, we have a relationship with these Powers. Technically, we live on borrowed land in their world. We depend upon them for the resources that help us sustain our lives. Many people I've encountered are drawn to the elements. They have a deep emotional response to the mountains, or fire, or to the oceans and seas. That's good. That's a good place to begin. It does not however, end there. It can't because our emotional responses in no way do anything to impact the relationship we have with the Powers. They can only spur us on into making those relationships better.

In reconstructing our traditions, on top of everything else we must re-learn, I think that we need to re-evaluate and reconsider our relationship with the Elemental Powers.

We've not been taught to reverence them. When I first wrote about this publicly, several people who contacted me privately were deeply offended by my belief (a belief shared by other ancestor and land workers) that the Elemental Powers are angry and have begun to lash out. It was very difficult for some readers to accept that these Powers may strike back by the only means available to them (i.e., natural disasters) and that we might well be reaping what we have well and truly sown. This implies that we have a debt to these Powers. It also implies that they are striking down the innocent as well as the guilty. It is not so much that I think these events are 'deserved,' but rather I think they are the logical consequences to a war of conquest that we as a species have waged for generations on the Powers of our world. It is the logical result of a world out of balance, of severed bonds, forgotten obligations, and a tremendous lack of mindful respect. Do I think that every single natural disaster or shift of tectonic plates is the Elemental Powers striking back at us? Of course not. I do think though, that we need to be mindful, because the elements can lash out and in many cases, they might well be considered right in doing so.

My colleague Sarenth said it best: "We are all connected in Wyrd, and when one thread moves to the detriment or betterment of many, the tapestry changes in reflection of it." It's crucial that we remember that. Reverencing the Elemental Powers is one more piece in restoring our sundered traditions. Our ancestors reverenced them. They dealt with them far more directly than we given the comforts of modernity have to do. It's time we returned to that mindset of respect and maybe even a little awe.

I'm admittedly new to really engaging with the elements as sentient powers so I will share what I do to honor them. Firstly I try to give before I take. I begin most of my rituals with making offerings to the ancestors. I include offerings to the Elemental Powers when I do so. I include them on my ancestral altar too. They are mentioned and honored with offerings every single time I mention my own ancestors. I also give offerings to my house vaettir (a catch-all Norse term for any spirit) pretty much whenever I cook anything and once a week set offerings outside for my land vaettir. In very simple, mundane terms, I go to the local park and pick up trash for a couple of hours once a month. I donate to various charities whose mission is protecting and conserving the land. I recycle, buy organic (as much as I can), and support my local farmers. I also pay attention to what is going on in my state, like fracking, and write to my state representatives to share my views. I do quite a bit of work with my local mountain. Moreover I talk to these spirits and I try to find out what they want and what is within my power to do for them. I try to be mindful as I make my way through my world. My own practice does tend to emphasize consciously and mindfully making offerings. The Havamal, part of the *Poetic Edda*, cautions the wise person to visit friends often and strengthen the bonds of friendship with frequent gift giving (stanza 41, Larrington translation). I see no reason why that shouldn't hold true with the Powers too. Now not everyone can do these specific things, but everyone can do something. It's a matter of discovering what that might be. Every little bit helps. It's part of the process of restoring balance in our world.

Quite often I have readers asking me what to do when even the idea of honoring the ancestors is an extremely uncomfortable one. My initial answer is simple: you persevere. I don't say that to be harsh. I say it because no practice comes all at once. It took me over ten years of constant work---at least ten years---to get a decent, consistent, ancestor practice going. It was hard! I had a level of discomfort and even aversion to it at first. More than once I wanted to scrap the whole thing and when I began fumbling my way into honoring the dead, it was more out of a sense of duty, of obligation, of the knowledge that it was something I should be doing (and with more than a little resentment at times) rather than any love for the ancestors or true comprehension of how vital that devotional connection is that motivated me. Nor was sorting myself out easy. It was worthwhile and it's enriched my spiritual life immeasurably but it was not in any way easy. In my case, the problem was largely that I was disconnected from my biological family. I resented for a very long time the idea of honoring them. I didn't know why it was important. I felt no particular connection, save with my maternal grandmother who was at times strongly present. It took as much sorting out. dealing with, and coming to terms with much of the discord with my living family as it did learning to engage with my dead family members. None of that was a quick process. So when I say 'persevere,' I'm speaking from very personal experience.

I think the main thing to understand if you want to do this and it makes you incredibly uncomfortable is that: (a) it doesn't mean you're doing anything wrong; and (b) it doesn't mean that you shouldn't honor your dead. There are a couple of reasons why one could have a very uncomfortable response to engaging with one's ancestors. The most common reason in my experience is that your relationship with your immediate family is unpleasant, hurtful, abusive, or just plain bad. In this case, it's completely understandable why even the idea of honoring one's kin---living or dead---would be unpleasant. Why would you, after all, honor people that hurt you? Nor is there an easy, one-size-fits-all fix.

Generally, when this comes up, I tell people that it is statistically impossible, as a friend once pointed out, for every single one of your ancestors (all the way back to the primordial ooze) to have been an unmitigated, abusive asshole. It's just statistically impossible. It's also statistically impossible that you don't have at least a couple of those types lurking about in your ancestral tree somewhere and probably more than a couple. This is true for all of us. What this means is that when your immediate blood kin were horrible or hurtful or whatever, there's a solution. I won't say it's a simple solution but it's the best and most workable one that I've found: go back farther. Go back farther in your lines until you find someone willing to engage with you in a healthy way, or with whom you can feel a connection. Sometimes it helps to start with personal heroes, or lineage ancestors (you're a mechanic, well, who were the leading innovators in your field that you respect---who happen to be dead---who taught you how to do what you do? Who helped and mentored you in your field? Who came before you in this work that, again, you respect and who are dead? These are your lineage ancestors and every field has them). Maybe you have friends or mentors who have died. They are ancestors too. It's a broad term after all and in the scope of ancestor work 'beloved dead' doesn't always mean 'blood kin.' So if you must, either start your ancestor practices far enough back that you avoid the recent generations that hurt you, or start with heroes, mentors, friends, etc. Eventually as you persevere, your practice will grow and with their help, you'll be able to address some of the issues, whatever they might be, making the practice of honoring your blood kin uncomfortable, and with hard work, you'll be able to develop a more organic practice. Stay the course and trust the process is how it was once put to me.

Now there are times where you will have to make the hard decision not to honor a specific branch of your dead. One of the things that many of us deal with is what to do when one part of your ancestry were slaves, and another slave owners; when one part were abusers, and the other those they abused, when one part attacked and slaughtered the other or engaged in other forms of cultural and religious devastation. This is not an easy question and like the above, there's no pat answer. In some cases, some of those ancestors may step forward wanting to make amends and pay their debt and help you. It's up to you whether or not you wish to accept. In other cases, they are just as miserable and nasty and hateful and cruel in death as they were in life and need to be exhumed from your venerations. Until they step up and do what they ought, they get nothing. You do not have to honor an ancestor who was horridly abuse to you in life. I've known more than one person who has made this choice and it has been an empowering one.

Sometimes, parts of your ancestral line may be closed to you because of some fear or shame in key ancestors in that particular line. Sometimes the blockage comes from the ancestor in question having deep shame still, even in death, sometimes it comes from their desire to protect you from something that they feel would come through them and with which they would not wish to have any decent person engage. For instance, for years, I was unable to get anywhere with my maternal father's line. No matter what I did, it was blocked: no connection, no information, nothing no matter how hard I tried. Frustrated, I finally brought it up in passing to an ancestor worker (a spiritworker who specializes in sorting out ancestor issues, dealing with the dead, and facilitating healthy relationships between ancestors and their descendants). This ancestor worker, without knowing any of the rumors that had circulated about my great-grandmother, pinpointed her story. My great-grandmother Edna had been an opera singer in late nineteenth century Baltimore. She had two little boys, and when they were six and nine respectively, she took them to a local park and left them there, saying she'd be right back. She never came back. The boys were put into foster care, which went badly for one of them, and years later when they found their mother again, she refused all but the most fleeting of contact with them. The six year old was my grandfather and this left a deep, deep wound in him, one that he carried into his marriage to my grandmother, and one that---after a great deal of suffering and in a time when one did not make this choice lightly---led to their divorce and to him disappearing from my family's history until close to his death decades later.

What the ancestor worker nailed was that my great-grandmother's father had been a sadist, cruel and brutal to his children. Edna was starting to see that coming out in herself with her children and did the only thing she felt she could do to spare them: she left them. Keep in mind, this was in the late 1800s, and she was a theatre performer. It wasn't likely that there were many agencies or social workers or facilities to help her. It wasn't after all, until 1874 that child abuse even became a recognized crime and then only after the ASPCA prosecuted the abuse of a small girl under regulations intended for the protection of farm animals. I suspect, given what I know about social history of even a few decades later, that there really were very few if any options open to her. Still, I found it very, very hard to come to terms with her actions even so, because I saw the resulting damage working its way down three generations. The thing that moved me was that the ancestor worker noticed something else. She said that Edna was too alienated and ashamed to make contact as an ancestor, but that she was standing guard, holding that line closed to me, so that her father would not be able to harass or harm later generations. Even as a spirit, her own wounds persisted and she was using them as valiantly as she could to help descendants with whom she could not effectively engage in life. That at least gave me something I could give a nod to and I was able to thank her for that, and begin the process of ancestor elevation. It wasn't long after that, when that particular ancestor line began opening up and now years later, it's a very important part of my working lineage.

So it may well be that it's one or two of your ancestors themselves who are making things difficult out of their own hurts which don't just necessarily go away when we die. This is one of the reasons that I'm grateful that in almost every case, one or two of your ancestors will step forward to sort of serve as gatekeepers, guardians, managers….they keep things running smoothly, get everybody else in order, and can really bring cohesion to an otherwise patchwork ancestral tree. If you know who your primary guardian ancestors are, then it's always a good idea to call upon them when issues arise, because it's their job to facilitate and organize on the 'ancestor' side of things and that goes a long way right there toward helping a person sort themselves out. Why bother, you might ask. Well, you get what you get. Your ancestors are your ancestors and keeping them healthy, helping them to heal, allowing them to function in ways that strengthen their wyrd benefits you as it will benefit your descendants. None of this is happening in a vacuum.

Now, there are occasionally---and I find this to be relatively rare---people who for whatever reason aren't called to honor their ancestors. In almost every case involved, this person was a spiritworker, and they were given over in service to a specific family of dead people. One person I know honors the wandering dead, another the transgender dead, and their ancestral obligations, with few exceptions, are all bound up in that specific Deity-inspired service. Even those few---and I want to make it clear these are specialized cases---who are tabooed from honoring their own dead, have some sort of devotional engagement with at least some of the dead some of the time.

I would also suggest making an offering, and I'd make it a personally significant one, to your Gods and Goddesses, to Whomever seems the most inclined to involve Him or Herself in ancestor related matters, and ask for help. Along with that, petition your ancestors, and go far back too. They have a vested interest in engaging properly with you and the burden for seeing that happen is not all on you. Like any relationship, it takes two to tango. There are two sides of the equation here and just as you are working to connect with them, so the reverse is very likely also true. Some at least, will be farther along in their ability to do this well so petition them too and ask for clear and consistent help.

Most of all, don't give up. We grow up and make our way forward in a culture antithetical to engaged devotion, reverence to the Gods and ancestors, and proper piety (or indeed any piety at all save the most shallow and self-serving of veneers). We are navigating the chasm of a disconnection with which many of our polytheistic ancestors at least, never had to contend. It's going to take time. It may be difficult. There may be grave wounds to heal. All of that is worth it though when those relationships become a strong and vital part of one's life. It is absolutely worth it and moreover, I believe it is a crucial curative to the disconnection and spiritual ills of our age.

Hero Cultus

One aspect of ancestor work that also doesn't get written or spoken about as much as it probably should is hero cultus. This was part and parcel of ancient ancestor veneration and often occurred on a community level. I've said it before though and I'll say it again: the ancestors are our best and strongest allies in this fight. They can help us get this restoration thing right. Our traditions were sundered. They were destroyed. Not only our traditions but any sense of lineage was torn away. That is such a horrific, collective, soul-deep devastation, a holocaust of such proportion that it's no wonder we're struggling. Our ancestors are there and they want to help us, but we lack the spiritual technology to figure out how to let them. We as a people have been disconnected so long, we don't realize we're disconnected.

When I talk and write about hero cultus, I think it's important to impact exactly what I mean by the term 'hero.' When I use that term, I mean the unique, superlative, elevated ancestors who are special carriers of strength and excellence, fortitude, and inspiration. Ancient or modern, maybe our ancestral heroes are exactly whom we ought to be calling for help on that. I would like to see offerings made, sacrifices done, all for the dead of our collective lineages, those that were sundered with the supremacy of monotheism. I would like to see the ancestors being honored and fed, and empowered in this restoration. But I would also like to see our traditional heroes venerated. This, I believe, is crucial.

In the meantime, that still leaves us with a disconnect. One of the areas that people seem to really, really struggle with is the restoration of our heroic cultus. This was not an uncommon facet of ancient polytheisms. I don't believe we have anything close to it in our modern world, save the Catholic cultus of saints. There's a big difference though, between saint cultus and ancient hero cultus. If I understand the theology correctly, Catholics venerate saints not only for the miracles they are believed to have performed, but as examples of how to live a good, decent, faithful life. That is not at all the case with ancient heroes.

Honoring heroes like Cú Chulainn, like Heracles, like Achilles, or even contemporary Heathen honoring of Saga heroes like Egil has absolutely *nothing* to do with their virtuous character. It has to do with their being larger than life figures, figures who performed remarkable, exceptional deeds, whose deeds affected their communities, who embodied in some way---to default to Greek---'arete.'

Arete is usually translated as 'excellence' and refers to glorious deeds performed by the would-be hero. The greatest of Greek epics, the work that influenced not only all of ancient Greek culture but Roman culture as well, Homer's *Iliad* was all about arete: distinction, fame, and glory. It had nothing to do with the behavior of Homeric heroes. Many of the most revered heroes were mighty warriors, which means they were highly trained killers, obsessed with personal glory, quite often willing to rape, pillage, and plunder nations. It is this quality of surmounting mediocrity, of setting in the threads of wyrd that which will stand as an incitement for later generations to excellence that leads to the veneration of heroes. That may hold true with modern heroes (like Malcolm X, Harriet Tubman, Gandhi, or Rosa Parks---all names recently brought up by modern polytheists as 'heroes') as well: it is not who they were so much as what they did with what they were that mattered.

There are also a couple of pre-requisites to being a hero:

1. You had to have lived at some point. You had to be *an actual person*---that is, an actual *living* person.

and

2. You had to do something worthy of veneration. You had to become part of your own mythic cycle. Your story had to become part of the mythic cycle of your people. It had to become fuel for future generations.

Part of the difficulty for us moderns may be the use of the term 'myth.' To paraphrase a popular film "I do not think that word means what you think it means." We use mythology to refer specifically to stories that are not true. The word itself implies something if not fictitious itself, then very, very close to it. It's something removed from our everyday reality. That is a post-Christian meaning. In ancient Greece, a culture deeply entrenched in heroic cultus, and from which the word 'myth' comes, it meant 'narrative, account, story.' There was no necessary implication of fiction. It was an account of something worth retelling. We are using the word today very, very differently than the cultures in which heroic cultus developed. This is, to be blunt, muddying the waters terribly.

Finally, perhaps the cultus of the dead is a buffer keeping out the frivolous. It forces one to root, and there is a segment of people who resent and resist that and all the responsibilities inherent in this restoration, that run fleeing from it. In every single traditional religion that I can think of that is the focus, the first focus to the point that we must sometimes go through our ancestors to reach the Gods. It opens up fighting the filter to a whole segment of people who think they have nothing left to offer there. Why? Because everyone has dead and as a beautiful Lithuanian proverb goes: "the souls of the dead are the protection of the living." With the heroic cultus, surely that would hold to an even greater degree. The purpose, the duty of many of these heroes was protecting and defending tradition. For that reason, it makes good sense to revive hero cultus within our respective traditions. It's an extension of ancestor work, in a polytheistic culture, almost an extension of civic ancestor work.

Yet another aspect of ancestor work, rather a corollary to hero cultus, is honoring one's lineage ancestors. When I use this term, I am referring to those honored predecessors in one's vocation: if you are a diviner, it's all the diviners that came before you; if you are an artist, it's all the artists that came before you; if you are a gardener, it's all the gardeners that came before you, and so on. Each vocation, each field has its lineage, its elders and honored predecessors. When we are working within a particular field, it's properly respectful and beneficial to pay homage to one's lineage. It creates a palpable sense of continuity that I believe is inherent in a well-functioning tradition. We are not yet at the point where we have intergenerational lines of mystery/wisdom/knowledge transmission within our traditions, but we're working on it and this is one aspect of 'filling in the gaps.'

99

I maintain a special part of my ancestor shrine dedicated just to my lineage ancestors: priests, shamans, diviners who came before me. I also honor any deceased elders of the traditions into which I've been initiated. Sometimes specific groups of ancestors can claim a person. I talked about this a little bit in passing earlier in the book, and I want to expand up on it briefly here. Some people are tapped for special obligations to groups of dead. For instance, I do a great deal of work in honoring the military dead. This means, among other things, that the military dead as a group have a special part of my shrine and that I have certain ongoing obligations, for instance, they receive special offerings on Veterans Day and Memorial Day and I have on more than one occasion been pushed to make pilgrimage to various battlefields, making offerings and communing with the dead there. It's a major part of my job as a spiritworker. I know several others who were tapped to speak for the transgender dead, one person who was tapped to speak for the deaf dead, one who honors the dead children in a particular cemetery, and so on.

Part of my work for the military dead is to encourage others to honor their military dead. We owe a debt to our soldiers and veterans. It is a debt that we may never repay. We owe a debt to those Vietnam vets who returned from war to be spat on. We owe a debt to those veterans who live on the street because their countries did nothing to help them transition back into civilian life. We owe a debt to those soldiers consumed by addiction because they've no other way of drowning out the voices of their fallen comrades. We owe a debt to those dead soldiers who fought and died in defense of ideals of freedom and self-determination: who died so that we would have the freedom to turn around and slander them.

Civilization was built on the backs of artisans and farmers. The mortar of that foundation was the blood of those willing to die to see the next generation thrive. That's what warriorship is all about: doing what is necessary to ensure that one's family, tribe, and civilization lives another day. Even when we miss the mark, even when we fail, on an individual level that sacrifice is worthy of respect. When we fail to honor our soldiers, and others who serve in the military, we dishonor every ancestor who ever had to take up arms to defend themselves, their livelihood, their families, children, countries, villages, and tribes. We dishonor all those who bled whether they wanted to or not, in order that we might have a chance for something better. The obligation of respect goes well beyond any ethnic, ideological, political, or social barriers. It's not about whether one agrees with the reason for the fight. But for those willing to stand up, march off and die, a significant number of our ancestors I might add, we wouldn't be here. We reap the benefits of those who came before us; therefore, it is right and proper that we honor them. We live in softer, not more enlightened times. We criticize their choices without any comprehension of the necessities involved. We all have ancestors who were warriors, every last one of us and we would not be here but for them.

Essentially, what it comes down to is this: honor your dead. Honor all your dead, not just the ones of whose professions you approved. Give thanks that you don't have to make the same sacrifices, or live the same life that they did. Give thanks that you don't have to fight and bleed and die for a future you never got to see. Give thanks and give them the common courtesy of respect for their part in your being here. War is a terrible thing, but warriorship is not. I can't speak for other groups of the dead---that's not my job---but I can be a voice for our warrior dead here and so, to the best of my ability I am. Honor them and pay attention in your ancestor work to whether or not you are called to also venerate a particular group of beloved dead. You may not be, but if you are, it is some of the most rewarding work possible. You will become a voice for the voiceless.

SUGGESTIONS

Go out and thank a Veteran today.

Go lay flowers on the grave of a fallen soldier.

> Make a donation to Wounded Warrior, Fischer House, or some other Veterans charity.
>
> Light a candle and thank the Gods you don't have to do what they did. Maybe even light a candle and thank your military dead for their service!

One other group of dead that I have been called more and more to honor are ballet dancers that inspired me when I was still working in that field. These women and some men (being a female dancer, I was far more interested in the stories of female dancers) inspired me, helped me to survive a difficult childhood, gave me passion and discipline and a desire to strive for something greater than myself regardless of the sacrifices involved. I worked hard for a career in ballet and while I had to retire due to injury at twenty-three, the lessons I learned in service to that most brutal of daemons served me well as a priest, spiritworker, shaman, and simple devotee of my Gods. I also honor the castrati on my altar. For those who may not know, until the mid-1800s, young boys with exceptional voices were often castrated before puberty and given special training to allow them to develop phenomenal skill and vocal range. The best went on to become the superstars of their day. That level of sacrifice and commitment inspires me, that discipline in the sake of beauty and art inspires me and so I venerate them along with the ballet dancers that kept me sane and kept me going through a very dark time in my life.

When I first wrote about this on my blog, a reader sent me the following questions and I'm going to repeat them here because I think having a clear example of how someone else does this type of thing, might prove helpful to those of you who also wish to honor specific, non-blood related groups of honored dead: "Would you be willing to blog about how you honor your ancestors of lineage (spiritual and artistic), and if it's not uncomfortable, share an idea or picture of what a shrine would be? Also, as an artist, do you have a conscious, intentional relationship with your creative/artistic daemon, or do you feel that doing the work is enough? What might such a practice look like?"

Those are really good questions and I had to sit back when I first read them and think long and hard. I've never actually talked about this part of my practice in any depth with anyone and to be fair, it's something that I myself am still developing. My ancestor practice is divided into three parts: blood and adoptive ancestors, spiritual lineage, artistic lineage. This latter group have become more and more important over the past couple of years as I've resolved much of the pain locked up in my retirement from ballet and as I've begun to paint and explore photography. I also had a series of powerful epiphanies last year where I realized how much I owed many of the dancers I include in my artistic lineage. It's really because of them that I not only survived, escaped a very stultifying home, but also that I gained the groundwork as a devotional polytheist. I learned the nuts and bolts of devotion and how to endure the ongoing process of transformation inherent in spiritual work. For me, that is not at all insignificant. So, how do I integrate all of this into my regular ancestor practice?

Well, with both my spiritual and my artistic lineages, I began by giving them each special sections of my ancestor shrine (which takes up the better part of a room in my home). For my spiritual lineage, I put photos of my deceased elders, images representing those too far back in the line to have photographs, this representing priestcraft, divinatory arts, shamanism. I have, for one of the traditions into which I've been initiated, my lineage written out and this I recite with prayers daily. I also make regular offerings.

For the artistic shrine, I honor two groups of people: ballet dancers who inspired me when I danced, and the operatic castrati. For the latter group, I have a period lithograph, and a couple of photocopied paintings of famous Castrati (no photos exist, it was too early; the first of my artistic lineage to be photographed in her prime was Fanny Cerrito, who was dancing at the height of her career when the daguerreotype was introduced). For my dancers it's a bit different.

I began with Anna Pavlova. She was the reason I began to dance, and a bio of her life was probably the most influential book on me ever. It kindled my passion for ballet. I tracked down original post cards from Imperial Russia with images of her dancing. These run between $20 and $150 (though a signed one can be in the thousands; mine are not signed) on today's market. They were put out as publicity images by the Maryinsky Theatre. I have ballet ephemera (old programs, a card someone wrote to her niece talking about seeing Pavlova dance, etc.) and I had these all nicely framed and hung by that part of my shrine. Then I turned to the second dancer who dramatically inspired me: Olga Spessivtseva (sometimes simplified to Spessiva). I did the same in terms of finding original images but here I could do one better. She is buried about 45 minutes away from where I live so I and a friend made a pilgrimage there two years ago. It took us awhile to find the Russian Orthodox cemetery and longer to locate her grave, but we did and left offerings and later installed a memorial to her on my shrine. Ballet is a lineage art, the tradition, choreographies, customs, and protocols are all passed down dancer to dancer, teacher to student. To honor them, as well as to respect my own small place in that lineage meant that I ought to be honoring their predecessors.

I began seeking out images for the dancers that inspired Pavlova and Spessivtseva, most notably Marie Taglioni (I have a newspaper clipping advertising her performances from early 1800s). I added images for Pierina Legnani, who revolutionized ballet technique, Mathilda Kchessinskaya, Olga Preobrajenska, several lithographs of Fanny Essler, Carlotta Grisi, Fanny Cerrito. I know my way around this lineage. When I watch a ballet being performed, I'm not just paying attention to the ballerina dancing a particular role *now*, I'm mentally placing her in a line of all the dancers to have performed that role back to the time the ballet was choreographed. When I recently saw *Sleeping Beauty* danced by the NYCB, I enjoyed the bluebird variation and connected that in my mind to Enrico Cecchetti, the first to perform it when the ballet was created, and that tied me to Pavlova and

Spessivtseva and indeed a whole generation of Imperial dancers, because he became a noted ballet master, and that tied me to the ballet russe for the same reason, which led to Balanchine who came from the Imperial school through the ballet russe and to my teacher and first director who trained as Balanchine's school....to me. That framework and understanding is first and foremost the basis for my interaction. Knowing my ballet history too allows me to pinpoint with absolute specificity how each of these women changed the face of their art. I honor male dancers more obliquely only because while working in the field, it was specifically female dancers---being one myself---from whom I drew the most inspiration and into whose roles I hoped to step.

For some of the 18th and early 19th century dancers, like La Camargo (who shorted her skirts to show the ankles and took the high heels off her shoes so she could showcase her jumps and intricate footwork; in the late 1800s Virginia Zucchi would repeat this with the Russian ballet, giving us the short ballet skirt that is now *de rigueur*) there weren't even really lithographs available. I had to look long and hard for an authentic image, rather than a photocopy of Camargo (photocopies are okay, but I really wanted something more authentic). I finally hit gold when I discovered tobacco cards. Up through the 1930s, many tobacco companies included novelty cards in their tobacco packs. A German company named Garbaty came out with a line of 'Famous Dancers,' which included Marie Camargo and other very, very early ballet stars. They seem to only showcase female dancers, but they have a broad array, including a drawing of an Etruscan dancer, a Greek dancer, an ancient Egyptian dancer which allows me to include representations for the ancient side of the linage on my shrine too. I did have to stop and think where to put some of these images because so much dance goes back to religious expression and ritual that I wondered if they could rightly be included in my spiritual lineage shrine, but then I figured that the modern dancers, while many like Preobrajenska, Pavlova, Spessivtseva to name a few, thought of their work as a spiritual vocation, just as many likely did not and best to give them their own space.

I like the images, but they aren't necessary for this work. I just really like them and they help me connect better just like having a bit of---oh, I don't know---rabbit fur might help one connect to the spirit of rabbit more effectively. This is a personal thing. If I were more aural, I might play ballet music for them (I do this for the castrati I honor). I tend toward the kinetic and visual though so for me, having authentic images, connects me to that time and place and that point in ballet lineage, and the women themselves.

I have rekindled, as an offshoot of my devotional practices, an interest in reading about ballet history and some of these famous dancers. I go to ballet more frequently now, even slowly do some of the basic exercises that once formed so much the warp and weft of my existence. I talk about them when people ask, and I venerate them, making offerings and prayers just as I would with my spiritual or blood/adopted ancestors. I find they are very present when I paint so when I engage in creative activities, I often do so as a way of honoring them. My practice here is still growing and I think it was one of the things that led me to take up painting and photography, given that I can no longer dance (this was also a blessing from Oshun but I think there's a connection there).

I haven't yet figured out how to honor the daemon of art...I know that I have to, even if simply in veneration and thanks for having fostered me, but that piece hasn't been given to me yet. I'm not worried. It will come and I think that developing a venerative practice for my artistic lineage is perhaps a good start to that.

Civic Ancestor Work

Hero and lineage cultus in many respects serve as a natural bridge between personal ancestor work and civic ancestor work. People ask me a lot what they can do to expand their ancestor practices. Hell, I ask myself the same question all the time! Once those connections start happening, it's easy to become very enthusiastic for the overall process and this is a good thing. So it's good and natural to wonder how you can expand what you're doing.

I want to do a quick and dirty breakdown of ancestor practices.

1. Firstly, there's the personal, domestic cultus: making offerings, maintaining a shrine, cooking for the dead, maybe studying genealogy. Things like showing filial piety by visiting graves, telling stories to your kids about their ancestors, encouraging ancestor awareness---all practices that increase your connection to your own personal dead, and which help you to foster and further your connections there.

2. But then there's this other, civic component, that isn't so much about your own ancestors, but about caring for your community's dead.

Hero cultus would fall somewhere in between. It makes sense that we forget about this: it's not like we live in a culture that has state supported ancestor or hero cultus. I didn't think anything of this at all until earlier this year. I was taking a student of mine to one of the local cemeteries to introduce her and to teach her the correct protocol for engaging with a cemetery and its dead. As she was walking around, this older guy comes scurrying over. He is chatty and asks me if I'm looking for anyone in particular. When I said I just liked to pay my general respects and wanted to show my friend the cemetery he got excited and asked if I was part of the local cemetery association.

Well, at that point, I was getting the sort of psychic poke from my ancestors that says "you may not be now, but you will be soon"! I got all the information from him and found out that the local historical society has a sub-committee dedicated to maintaining the local cemeteries, fixing headstones, holding educational events and tours, and otherwise increasing local knowledge about the many cemeteries in my area as well as making sure that they're properly cared for. I'd lived in my little town for years but hadn't any inkling that this existed.

I started attending the monthly meetings and took on a couple of little projects and…felt my own ancestors responding positively. It's not as though any of the work I have slowly started to do with the cemetery committee benefits them directly but they very clearly approve. It took me awhile to parse out why and the closest I can describe it is that it's the civic equivalent of filial piety and that this is a necessary component of ongoing ancestor work.

What's nice about this is that you don't have to be a medium to do this work really, really well and for those who may be struggling with their personal ancestor work (it can take some time when there are family issues and what family doesn't have issues?), this can be a really good way to engage.

So I plod along with this doing what I can. It's another aspect of ancestor work. Here are a few more things, some already discussed, some not, that you can do to augment your ancestor work:

1. Make a donation to a charity of which you feel your ancestors might have approved.

2. Go visit a local cemetery. Walk around and if you see flowers or flags that have fallen over on specific graves, right them. If you see a grave overgrown, pick those weeds. If you see untidiness, put it into order. Better yet, start a project and invite others to get involved. Work with your local cemetery committee, guild, or association to keep your local cemeteries in good repair.

3. Go to an estate planner or attorney and put your own will and final testament in order. You may not be planning on dying any time soon, but accidents happen and part of honoring the dead, is realizing that you have an obligation to care for the living too and that includes making sure that your family, children, friends, and other loved ones who will be left behind when you die have as easy and painless a

108

time as possible where paperwork is concerned. Take care of those you love; take care of those for which you're responsible. Living or dead, it doesn't matter.

4. If you learned a skill from a deceased relative---woodworking, or taking care of your car, or cooking, or just a series of recipes, or knitting socks for that matter---teach it to someone else. If you have children or nieces and nephews, and they're willing, teach them. If not, just pass that knowledge on and as you do so, talk about the person who taught you and all you learned from him or her. There's a saying in Lukumi that whenever an elder dies, an entire world dies with him or her. That is so, so true both with respect to religious rituals and knowledge and in crafts, skills, experience, and learning. Preserve what you can by telling their stories, teaching what you have learned. This is ancestor work, creating those inter-generational links through which knowledge, culture, and wisdom may be transmitted.

A Samhain Dream

My adopted mom once shared a beautiful dream that she had, a dream that we both felt was more than just an ordinary one. She was an immensely devout devotee of Loki. He was her sustenance, the witness to her life, her God, her Lord, her deepest love. Throughout her life, He guided and cared for her in a way that she felt palpably all the way to the end of her life. I was recently looking over some letters that she had sent me, for we often exchanged old-fashioned correspondence, yes, actually using pen, careful script, and reams of pretty stationary! I have saved each and every one. With the coming of Samhain and Winternights, I was struck once again by the power of this dream that she seemingly so long ago shared with me, and so I shall share it with you now and beg her indulgence for doing so. It was written at a point shortly before her death and with the approach of this winter's season, I have been thinking about that quite a lot,

109

mourning the passing of all those that I have loved and celebrating the time we shared together. I have been remembering this person in particular, this witness to my life, and all the many things that I learned from her about living rightly.

I shall allow my mom to speak with her own words:

"In my dream, I was remembering my life, or rather re-experiencing it---not the incidents, so much as the emotions: my heart's life, as it were. And Loki came behind me, took my forearms and crossed them on my chest (like statues of Pharaohs in ancient Egyptian art) and said something. The closest it can be put into words is this: "'I wrap the cloak of your life around you. It can all fall in place and be quiet now---you've done all the joys, all the sorrows. You're done trying. You can rest now---I wrap the cloak of your life around you.'

"It was a side of Loki I'd never seen. The closest I can come to explaining is that He was Sigyn's husband and Hela's Father: a huge, serene, golden presence, full of both vitality and calm.

"In the dream, the cloak that Loki formed by my life was large enough to cover me. I had enough 'memories of the heart' that they could weave themselves, or be woven by the Norns, into a cloak that fit. I am speechless with this gift. I love Him so much. If I could sing, I'd sing the Magnificat for Him. This dream was my gift and blessing."

It took her a long time to realize that this was her shroud; that, apparently, we work on our shroud throughout our lifetimes. Andvari said something similar to me once, that we are all craftsman: our life and wyrd is our art. It is a thing to contemplate as the dark time of winter draws closer, the time when the Wild Hunt rides, when the ancestors clamor for acknowledgement (if we haven't already been doing this regularly). It is a time to contemplate our own

110

progress on our 'shrouds.' What are we weaving into our lives? What kind of cloak will warm and sustain us when we pass from the realm of Midgard?

Who has contributed the threads? What kind of memories of the heart do we carry within our souls?

Honoring the dead is about honoring life too, that we may learn from their mistakes, celebrate their victories, reap the benefits of their care and wisdom and in doing so make our own lives, and the lives of those we touch, better: mentally, emotionally, physically, and spiritually. It's about embracing life at its fullest and learning to live with a vibrant integrity each and every day of our lives.

I have often thought in my own devotions that I would like the totality of my life, when the time of its ending comes, to have been lived in such a way that I may hand it over to Odin as a gift and that He may find it a worthy offering. That is my goal, something I strive for each and every day. It never occurred to me that in being given the opportunity to do so, I was weaving a gift for myself as well.

We are blessed in what we do. In living and dying we are blessed. In the struggle of weaving our lives and our wyrd we are blessed. I think it's up to us to work hard at not forgetting that.

Recommended Resources

Sadly, there aren't many I'd recommend that I haven't already mentioned throughout the course of this book. I was hoping to find more useful resources but that has not been the case. Perhaps some of you will have useful things to recommend and if so, I encourage you to contact me, to share them with your friends, to talk about how you honor your dead, and to work together to do all this ancestor 'stuff' better.

Firstly, many find it helpful to do genealogy. There are several good sources:

> ➢ ancestry.com
> ➢ rootsweb.net
> ➢ familysearch.com

You can get your DNA tested and learn your haplo-group at www.genebase.com. There are other organizations that do this type of testing too and some even test for Neanderthal DNA. This type of testing is especially good for those who know absolutely nothing about their ancestry. It can at least give you regions in which to start. The downside is that women need to have a male relative also test in order to trace their paternal lines. (This is not discrimination! It has to do with pure genetics: women don't have an XY chromosome).

To make sure your own wishes are carried out, this is a great resource: funeralplan.com.

Here is an excellent resource from a conjure perspective on ancestor work: readersandrootworkers.org/wiki/Ancestors.

If any of you live near a Chinatown, there are often shops that either specialize in offerings for the dead, or that carry things that your dead might like. There's paper money for instance, called hell money, that many ancestors adore. You burn it in offering. We know it's not real money, but perhaps because it's made specifically as currency for the dead, they seem to really appreciate it.

There are a couple of books I recommend:

> *Calling to Our Ancestors* by Sarenth Odinsson, forthcoming through Asphodel Press
> *Crossing the River* by Camilla Laurentine, forthcoming
> *Weaving Memory* by Laura Patsouris, available at amazon.com or asphodelpress.com.

The thing to remember is that the key to good ancestor work is consistency. Keep on keeping on and trust your instincts. Now that you've established this relationship, you'll be going hand in hand with your ancestors in allowing it to evolve. I wish you luck and many blessings in this work.

A Memorial to My Mother
written on her birthday 5/4/13

Today is my adopted mom's birthday, or would have been if she were still alive. She died in 2010. I loved this woman and she loved me with a ferocity that once led her to challenge Odin on my behalf. We love each other still of course, mother and daughter, one dead, one living bound through the grace of ancestor veneration. You'd think being a shaman it would be easy to deal with death, to accept that the spirit lives on. It's not. Her death still hurt terribly, beyond anything I have the verbal capacity to describe. Death carried away my joy, and it took me a very long time to find bring myself back. She helped with that too. Her story, the parts we wrote together, and the parts she shared with me from her life before we met, are etched in my heart. I am defined by this woman: there is before she died and after. But she was my mother and that, I think, is as it should be.

Through the first part of her adult life, my mom lived in Basel. She had attended the music conservatory there, taught music less than a block from the school (if I recall correctly, on Einhorn Str.---her building had a unicorn on it, small and tasteful and one could just see the top of the piano through the window). She and her partner lived in Basel, and when he died she left that city for good. She said she couldn't stand it, that every cobblestone echoed his presence and it hurt too much to see the city go on when he wasn't there as well. It held too many memories. I get this.

My mom, when I knew her, lived in Carmel. I will never go back there. The city holds the breath and shadow of her memory but she is not there and how *dare* it exist without her. How *dare* it go on when she no longer lives. It angers me that the city continues….in the aching world of my heart it has no *raison d'être* now that she is gone. I finally understand full well why she only once returned to Basel after her lover's death, and then only out of stark necessity and for as brief a time as possible. Some things even time cannot rid of pain.

Her partner was a pianist and a well known linguist. He

115

died of lung cancer and the last six weeks of his life, on his death bed, he taught himself Italian. He was reading Dante in the original before he died. When he died, my mom was teaching a class. Her friend came to the window. She looked out, saw her friend's face and said her partner's name. Her friend nodded and my mother died inside a little. She stopped eating for a time, shaved her head and shared her grief with the other woman he loved---they were polyamorous in a time when no one spoke of it; my mom was poly before poly was cool. I had dinner once: her, me, and his spirit as present as if he were there in the flesh, almost, and so I met the man she loved and who loved her in return. I took cigars to his grave site once. He liked to smoke.

Last night I was feeling so raw. I couldn't figure out why but I was feeling so fragmented. It took me awhile to realize that today was my mom's birthday. My partner called me and when he heard my voice and found out why I hurt so, asked me to tell him about her, to tell him her stories, of the times we shared together. So I did and it helped and through my words and tales one who is so important to me now, came to know at least a little, the one who restored me to life. There are many ways to give life after all, expelling a child from the womb is only one of them.

My mom was an atheist for a long time. The pain of the world hurt her terribly, broke something vital in her soul when first she experienced it. She told me once she'd been so isolated as a child, and in her first experience with the anguish of the world she was like Siddhartha. Nothing was ever the same for her again. Humanity appalled her. She was an atheist for years until somehow someone introduced her to the Norse Gods. She was dubious but something must have pinged for she started exploring it. She felt a strong, very strong draw to Loki. One night, as she related to me, shortly after this introduction, she lit a candle and challenged Him bitterly to prove His existence to her. (Hubris she would later admit, but at the time she knew no better.) That night, the blankets were ripped off her bed and she was yanked out of the bed and onto the floor by Loki. That direct experience changed everything for her.

She could speak to bees and dogs and they would listen and sometimes she understood when they spoke back. She could speak to and understand cats but they disdained her counsel and seldom obeyed. She was terrified of horses---except Sleipnir---because she could not read them, but knew they were intelligent, and that they knew she couldn't hear their thoughts....they were unpredictable to her and this frightened her. She once braved two very large horses so my god daughter---quite small at the time---could feed apples to a friend's horse. He was in a stable shared with several other riders. A big horse was being groomed by a woman. As my god daughter held the apple up to horse #1, horse #2 butted in to get his share. She fed him some, so he wouldn't feel left out and only later did we realize she'd fed someone else's horse. I remember my mother's face, white as a sheet, as she held my god daughter's hand, inches away from those two horses. That's when I learned of her fear. She was also afraid of alligators but this was far less troublesome!

She was a very humble, very stubborn, very fierce powerhouse. She taught me more about devotion than I ever thought possible and did much to heal what was then a very broken and scarred heart. I can love because of her, but more than that, I can find some measure of joy in living because of her. She was a miracle worker in my world, and she never would believe the number of lives she touched and transformed. My House honors her as a sancta and I am not the only Heathen to do so. She of course would be appalled and say such veneration is far more rightly given to Sigyn.

I miss her. Every day I miss her. She had a high pitched Basel accent and whenever I hear a woman with that accent, I want to cry and I want to smile at the same time. I watched the movie *Les Miserables* recently and almost had to turn it off. Anne Hathaway, when her character has her head shorn looked so much like my mom, and the tale of that character is one of such sadness, degradation, and grief. I found myself weeping and it was solely that I could not look at it and not see my mom in Hathaway's high-cheekboned face, short hair, and huge, huge eyes. She translated Midgard for me, this woman fluent in seven languages. She translated Midgard

117

for me and taught me to navigate a language of being as unfamiliar and alien to me as ancient Greek had once been to her. She gave me fragments of knowledge, taught me to appreciate the grace-notes of Midgard, as she called them. Most of all, she loved me as only a mother could. I have been very blessed in my life. I know this.

So today I remember my adopted mother.
May she ever and always be hailed.
Ashe.

Remember

It is never too late to honor your dead.
It is never too early to begin.
Do not worry
about whether you will do it right.
Do not worry
whether you do as I do,
or that ancestor worker over there,
or this one here.
It does not matter.
The work will teach you.
Your own dead will school you
in whatever protocols they desire.
Those gathered in the footprints
of your blood, and bone, and memory
are for you.
Seek them out.
Honor them.
Never stop.
they will fill your life with blessings
and in turn
you will fill their death
with satisfaction.
It is the way of things.
Tend your dead
and let them tend you
in return.
It is right.
It is proper.
Fas.
Set aside your fear.
Set aside your excuses
Conquer your indolence,
and get to work.
Your dead are waiting.

"I freed thousands of slaves; I could have freed thousands more if they knew they were slaves."

(Harriet Tubman)

About Galina Krasskova

Galina Krasskova is a Heathen (Norse polytheist) and has been a priest of Odin and Loki since the early nineties. Originally ordained in the Fellowship of Isis in 1995, Ms. Krasskova also attended the oldest interfaith seminary in the U.S. – the New Seminary where she was ordained in 2000 and where she worked as Dean of Second Year Students for the Academic year of 2011-2012. She is the head of House Sankofa, a member of the Thiasos of the Starry Bull, a member of Asatru in Frankfurt (Frankfurt am Main, Germany), the First Kingdom Church of Asphodel (MA), the American Academy of Religion, and the Religious Coalition for Reproductive Choice. Beyond this, she took vows as a Heathen gythia in 1996 and again in 2004.

Ms. Krasskova holds diplomas from The New Seminary (2000), a B.A. in Cultural Studies with a concentration in Religious Studies from Empire State College (2007), and an M.A. in Religious Studies from New York University (2009). She's presented at prestigious academic conferences including those held at Harvard, Santa Barbara University, and Ohio State University. Her Master's thesis, titled "Race, Gender, and the Problem of 'Ergi' in Modern Heathenry" explored concepts of gender roles within contemporary Heathen ritual structure and their impact on contemporary ideological fault lines. She is currently pursuing Ph.D. in Classics.

An experienced diviner, ordeal master, and conjure woman, her primary interests are in restoring Heathenry as an indigenous religion, developing a thriving ancestor cultus, devotional work, and the reconstruction of Northern Tradition shamanism. Her book *The Whisperings of Woden* was the landmark first devotional text to be written in modern Heathenry. In addition to her own books, she's also contributed extensively to Raven Kaldera's shamanism series.

Ms. Krasskova co-hosts (with Dionysian and author Sannion), a bi-monthly radio podcast: Wyrd Ways Radio. She has a variety of published books available running the gamut from introductory texts on the Northern Tradition, to books on runes, prayer, and devotional practices, with more books on the way. She is also the managing editor of *Walking the Worlds*, a new journal focusing on contemporary polytheism and spiritwork (walkingtheworlds.wordpress.com). While very busy with teaching and school, she does also occasionally lecture around the country on topics of interest to contemporary Heathenry and polytheisms.

For more information, please contact her directly at krasskova@gmail.com.

Other Titles by Sanngetall Press

He is Frenzy: Collected Writings on Odin by Galina Krasskova

Transgressing Faith: Race, Gender, and the Problem of 'Ergi' in Modern American Heathenry by Galina Krasskova

Consuming Flame: A Devotional Anthology for Loki and His Family by Galina Krasskova

Dancing in the House of the Moon: A Devotional for the Moon God Mani edited by Galina Krasskova

Also by Galina Krasskova

Numinous Places (blurb.com)

Neolithic Shamanism (Inner Traditions, with Raven Kaldera)

Essays in Modern Heathenry (Asphodel Press)

Runes: Theory and Practice (New Page Books)

Exploring the Northern Tradition (New Page Books)

Northern Tradition for the Solitary Practitioner (New Page Books, with Raven Kaldera)

Feeding the Flame: A Devotional to Loki and His Family (Asphodel Press)

The Whisperings of Woden (Asphodel Press)

Root, Stone, and Bone: Honoring Andvari and the Vaettir of Money (Asphodel Press, with Fuensanta Arismendi)

Sigyn: Our Lady of the Staying Power (Asphodel Press)

Sekhmet: When the Lion Roars (Asphodel Press)

Into the Great Below: A Devotional for Inanna and Ereshkigal (Asphodel Press)

A Child's Eye View of Heathenry (Spero Press)

Honoring Sigyn: the Norse Goddess of Constancy (Spero Press)

Sigdrifa's Prayer: An Exploration and Exegesis (Asphodel Press)

Skalded Apples: A Devotional Anthology for Idunna and Bragi (Asphodel Press)

Walking Toward Yggdrasil (Asphodel Press)

Full Fathom Five (Asphodel Press)

Day Star and Whirling Wheel (Asphodel Press)

Made in the USA
Middletown, DE
17 June 2015